W9-DGE-015

George Moore

GEORGE MOORE:
The Artist's Vision,
The Storyteller's Art

Janet Egleson Dunleavy

Lewisburg
BUCKNELL UNIVERSITY PRESS

© 1973 by Associated University Presses, Inc.

Associated University Presses, Inc.
Cranbury, New Jersey 08512

Library of Congress Cataloging in Publication Data

Dunleavy, Janet Egleson.
  George Moore.

  Bibliography: p.
  1. Moore, George, 1852–1933.
PR5043.D8   823'.8   75-125793
ISBN 0-8387-7757-0

Printed in the United States of America

Contents

Chronology

1852   Born 24 February, eldest son of George Henry Moore, M.P. for Mayo, and Mary Blake, at Moore Hall. Name: George Augustus Moore.

1858–
1861   Father not returned to Parliament, racing stables built up at Moore Hall; Croaghpatrick trained, wins Stewards Cup.

1861–
1868   Attends St. Mary's College, Oscott, near Birmingham with two-year interruption, 1863–1865, because of ill health; withdraws without completing curriculum.

1868–
1870   Father reelected to Parliament; family takes home in South Kensington, London; Moore studies for army examinations and attends evening classes in drawing and painting at South Kensington Museum, also meets Jim Browne, painter, and is introduced to betting circles of St. John's Wood.

1870   Death of George Henry Moore; decision to pursue career in painting leads to more concentrated study of art.

1873   Arrives Paris March 13; enrolls in classes first

at Beaux Arts, then at Salon Julien; meets Lewis Hawkins.

1874   Brief return to London, takes studio in Cromwell Mews, enrolls in Barthe's classes, meets Whistler. [According to Joseph Hone, Moore's biographer, and the bibliography compiled by I. A. Williams, published in 1921, a play, *Worldliness,* was published in London this year, but no other record of it appears to exist.]

1875   Auction of Impressionist paintings, Hotel Drouot, Paris.

1876–   Abandons idea of career in art; meets Bernard
1878   Lopez, who introduces Moore to Montmartre café society, symbolist poets, naturalist writers, impressionist painters.

1878–   First serious attempts to develop career as
1883   writer: Two volumes of poetry (*Flowers of Passion, Pagan Poems*), one play (*Martin Luther,* written in collaboration with Bernard Lopez), short stories, reviews, and short articles published in England. Move to London from Paris made necessary by diminished rent receipts from Moore Hall estate; Land League activities require closer supervision of Irish property.

1883   First publication of *A Modern Lover; Les Cloches de Corneville* produced in London with lyrics in English by George and Augustus Moore. Beginning of Moore's battle with the circulating libraries.

1884   First publication of *A Mummer's Wife* (published late in year; title page gives date of publication as 1885).

1885   *Literature at Nurse* attacks circulating libraries.

1886   First publication of *A Drama in Muslin; Terre d'Irlande (Parnell and His Island)* published in France.

1887   First publication of *A Mere Accident; Parnell and His Island* published in English.

1888   First publication of *Confessions of A Young Man* and *Spring Days.*

1889   *Mike Fletcher* published.

1891   Previously published essays and sketches revised and collected in book form under title *Impressions and Opinions;* first publication in book form of *Vain Fortune* (previously serialized).

1893   First publication of *Modern Painting,* including pieces previously printed in periodicals; production and publication of three-act play, *The Strike at Arlingford;* "Passages from the Life of a Workgirl," early version of *Esther Waters,* serialized in *Pall Mall Gazette.*

1894   First publication of *Esther Waters.*

1895–
1898   Death of Mary Blake Moore; publication of *Celibates* and *Evelyn Innes* reveals influence of Dujardin, interest in Wagner.

1899–
1901   Joins Lady Gregory, W. B. Yeats, and Edward Martyn in Irish Literary Theatre; moves to Dublin; develops interest in work of Gaelic League. *The Bending of the Bough* (rewriting of Edward Martyn's *The Tale of a Town*) pro-

duced and published; *Diarmuid and Grania*
(written in collaboration with W. B. Yeats)
produced; *Sister Teresa* (sequel to *Evelyn Innes*) published.

1902– *An T-Úr-Gort, Sgealta,* signed Seorsa O Morda
1903 (Moore's name in Irish) published; first book
publication in English of *The Untilled Field*
(stories written for *An T-Úr-Gort,* some previously printed in *New Ireland Review*). Disenchantment with Gaelic League; end of direct
role in building of Irish national theater.

1905 First publication of *The Lake;* accepts appoint-
ment to post of High Sheriff of Mayo.

1906– First book publication of *Memoirs of My Dead*
1911 *Life* (pieces previously printed in *Dana*) and
The Apostle (expanded from scenerio printed
in *English Review*); work on *Hail and Farewell.*

1911– Move to London; first publication of *Hail*
1914 *and Farewell;* production and publication of
Esther Waters: A Play and *Elizabeth Cooper.*

1916 First publication of *The Brook Kerith.*

1918 First publication of *A Story-Teller's Holiday.*

1919– First book publication of *Avowals* (pieces pre-
1920 viously printed in periodicals).

1921 First publication of *Heloise and Abelard.*

1923 Fire destroys Moore Hall.

1924 First publication of *Conversations on Ebury
Street;* also *Pure Poetry, The Pastoral Loves of
Daphnis and Chloe,* and *Perronik the Fool.*

1926– First publication of *Ulick and Soracha* and *The*

1927   *The Making of an Immortal.*

1930   First publication of *Aphrodite in Aulis;* also *A Flood, The Talking Pine.*

1933   First publication of *A Communication to My Friends;* death of George Augustus Moore.

Note: No attempt has been made to include in this Chronology either a complete record of Moore's essays, sketches, stories, and reviews published in periodicals or subsequent editions (reprints or revisions) of books after the first: for such information see *A Bibliography of George Moore* by Edwin Gilcher (DeKalb, Illinois: Northern Illinois University Press, 1970).

Introduction

To study the writings of George Moore, as Graham Hough has observed, is to examine "a panoramic view of the formation of a taste and attitude of all the various aesthetic and social influences that helped to shape it." His career, according to Malcolm Brown, was "an incomparable aesthetic journey, ranging more widely than the careers of Shaw, or Bennett, or Wells, or even Joyce and Yeats, though he did not always return from his expeditions as enriched as they." At one time or another during his sixty-year writing career, to be sure, Moore seriously considered himself a Pre-Raphaelite, a naturalist, a decadent, and an impressionist. To the end he was still seeking, still experimenting, still changing: his last literary style establishes his place among twentieth-century authors of the poetic-symbolist novel.

For the most part, Moore acknowledged the influences that helped to shape his literary career. In letters and autobiographical writings he praised in turn such disparate figures as Shelley, Pater, Flaubert, Turgenev, Zola, Baudelaire, Degas, Manet, and Edouard Dujardin. And in the literary salons of London, in the studios and cafés of Paris, in the drawing rooms of Dublin, he met other men and women whose ideas he adopted—sometimes giving credit, sometimes not.

It is not by accident that painting and writing, painters and writers, all contributed to Moore's development as a literary artist. The nineteenth century, as Robert Louis Stevenson once observed, was "an age of the optic nerve in literature." At its inception, Wordsworth and Coleridge sought to reinterpret the natural world through fresh observations of reality. Painting, sculpture, and poetry were interrelated in the work of the Pre-Raphaelites. The French novelists, notebook in hand, based their novels on eyewitness accounts of the visible world. Literary impressionists adapted ideas developed by the impressionist painters. And a "painterly" style was consciously cultivated by Henry James and Marcel Proust, as well as by lesser writers of the period.

While Moore's literary achievements did not, of course, match that of James or Proust, his connection with painters and painting was, in many respects, more personal and more meaningful. Moore had studied art seriously in London and Paris before he began to write. For almost ten years he had convinced himself, his family, and many of his friends that he was indeed an artist whose efforts one day would be worth preserving. By the time his own critical judgment forced him to admit that he lacked sufficient talent for such a career, he had acquired considerable training in the philosophy and methods of several different schools of art. Even when he turned to writing, as he often acknowledged, he could not create what he could not visualize. In his early fiction, therefore, it is not surprising to find well-known portraits and landscapes used metaphorically, as well as descriptive passages taken from art, not life. In later years Moore sometimes asked friends—many of them prominent painters—to sketch out a scene for him, that he might put it into words. A significant characteristic of his work throughout his career is its dependence on the visual arts. The language of painting pervades his writings; its theories inform his techniques.

Moore's tastes in art, however, unlike those of Proust and James, changed frequently. The changes were reflected in whatever he wrote. The result is a body of work which seems to lack unity of form, style, theme, characterization. Critics may speak, and do, of a Jamesian or Proustian passage; it is not correspondingly possible to describe a page as "typical of Moore." One contemporary observed that Moore had at least seven different styles; Oscar Wilde accused him of conducting his education in public, book by book; his brother, Maurice Moore, simply threw up his hands and said that George had no style at all.

Moore's early fiction, for example, has the atmosphere of the Academy. Landscapes are painted in trite imitation of Academy models; women strike poses, wear clothing, and have figures reminiscent of Botticelli and Rossetti. Later, Degas and Manet serve. Early descriptive passages abound in reference to light and shadow. Color is used to establish mood and setting in later

works. In the novels beginning with *The Lake,* published originally in 1905, there is a gradual shift of
emphasis from the nature of the object or person perceived to the nature of the perceptions of the observer.
By the time *The Brook Kerith* appeared in print in
1916, Moore, a poor stylist in his early writing, had
learned to use prose in a sophisticated, symbolist
manner.

   Moore's contribution to literature, however, is significant not only because it reflects trends in the development of prose fiction from 1873 to 1933, nor just
because it illustrates the application of theories and
techniques derived from the visual arts. Indeed, his
work was widely read and acclaimed for its own sake
during his lifetime. In 1885 he successfully challenged
the authority of the circulating libraries, thought to be
absolute; his books were sold without their sanction.
In 1899 when W. B. Yeats and Edward Martyn sought
his support for their Irish theater, they knew that to
win over George Moore was to gain the support of the
author of *Esther Waters,* a man of influence and experience. In 1912 the publication of *A George Moore
Calendar,* a collection of quotations from his works for
each day of the year, testified to his continuing popu-
larity. Almost all his books, including his autobiographical writings, remained in print throughout his lifetime.
Nine years before his death in 1933, the Carra collected
edition, an authorized edition of his works, was completed; within four years after his death the Ebury
edition was published. Moore's literary reputation during his lifetime also can be assessed from the fact that

before 1933 he was the subject of five book-length studies and numerous articles and essays written by others. Indeed, when one English publisher proposed a series that would examine the works of major living authors, George Moore was named among the first six. By the time Moore died, just a few weeks before his eighty-first birthday, he had published under separate titles twenty-one volumes of prose fiction, nine plays, eleven volumes of essays and autobiographical sketches, and two volumes of poetry. Many had been reissued in revised form, some with new titles. (Some critics regard his extensively revised novels as new works.) Books and articles concerned with his literary achievement continued to appear during the five years following his death, from 1933 to 1938, while his own books continued to attract a reading public. If critical attention and readership declined after 1939, World War II probably was partly to blame. Wartime restrictions placed many titles by many authors on out-of-print lists.

Interest in the works of George Moore was renewed early in the 1950s. Within ten years, four new full-length studies appeared, and three novels, one volume of short stories, and several volumes of autobiographical writings were reprinted. Today, another ten years have passed, and as more and more students of literature are examining Ireland's extraordinary contribution to English poetry, drama, and fiction, George Moore is receiving increasing attention. Critics now note that the Irishness of his work, long ignored or denied, deserves reconsideration. And a study of his Irish sources, themes, and characters, never fully explored, might well lead to a new critical view of his varying style, his experiments in technique, and his influence on the works of others. In the introduction to a collection of essays first published in 1968, *George Moore's Mind and Art,* Graham Owens raises significant questions:

> In what ways did he affect the work of Charles Morgan and David Garnett? How great was his impact on the Irish short story, on James Joyce, Frank O'Connor, Liam O'Flaherty, Sean O'Faolain, Edna O'Brien, and James Plunkett? Did *The Untilled Field* influence *Dubliners* in any significant way? Did *Vain Fortune* have any effect on the shape of "The Dead"? Did *The Old Wives' Tale* owe to *A Mummer's Wife* only its original inspiration and its environment? . . . What precisely was his influence on . . . later experimenters, what was his contribution to novelistic vision?

While the following brief introduction to the prose, drama, and poetry of George Moore cannot hope to answer such questions, perhaps—in repeating these and raising others—it may help to encourage long-overdue serious study of his work.

Meanwhile, as Edwin Gilcher points out in his admirable new work, *A Bibliography of George Moore* (Northern Illinois University Press, 1970), Joseph Hone's *Life of George Moore* (London, 1936) is an indispensable aid for which the present generation of readers can be grateful. For biographical and critical details of Moore's life and career, I am also indebted to Joseph Hone, *The Moores of Moore Hall* (London, 1939); John Freeman, *A Portrait of George Moore in a Study of His Work* (London, 1922); Maurice Moore, *An Irish Gentleman: George Henry Moore*

(London, 1912) ; Malcolm Brown, *George Moore: A Reconsideration* (Seattle, 1955) ; Charles Morgan, *An Epitaph on George Moore* (New York, 1935) ; Humbert Wolfe, *George Moore* (London, 1931) ; Georges-Paul Collet, *George Moore et la France* (Geneva, 1957) ; Nancy Cunard, *GM: Memories of George Moore* (London, 1956) ; Jean C. Noel, *George Moore: L'Homme et l'Oeuvre (1852–1933)* (Paris, 1966) ; Helmut Gerber, ed., *George Moore in Transition* (Detroit, 1968) ; and to a lesser degree to many other books and articles. I have also consulted, of course, George Moore's less reliable letters and autobiographical writings. In addition, it has been my good fortune to have been able to seek the help of Dr. John Langan of Castlebar, County Mayo, and Philip O'Reilly of Claremorris, County Mayo, whose memories and whose own investigations have been of great value and interest.

For encouragement and support in this and other work related to George Moore, I should like to express my thanks to Professor David Greene of New York University, Professor Herbert Weisinger of the State University of New York at Stony Brook, Professor Richard Kain of the University of Louisville, Professor Marilyn Gaddis Rose of the State University of New York at Binghamton, and Professor Gareth W. Dunleavy of the University of Wisconsin-Milwaukee.

George Moore

1

Cultural Background and Intellectual Milieu

Because George Moore was so much a part of his age, because he was so indebted to the people around him for what he became, no analysis of his literary achievement is complete without a summary of what he inherited from his family and what he absorbed from his social and cultural milieu. In *Confessions of a Young Man*—Moore's early autobiographical novel revised as fictionalized autobiography—he writes:

> I came into the world apparently with a nature like a smooth sheet of wax, bearing no impress, but capable of receiving any. Nor am I exaggerating when I say I think I might equally have been a Pharaoh, an ostler, a pimp, an archbishop; and that in the fulfillment of the duties of each a certain measure of success would have been mine.

The truth of these lines is obscured by their outrageous claims, so characteristic of Moore's first-person statements. Pharaoh? Ostler? Pimp? Archbishop? George

Moore as created by George Moore was a character designed to shock and to irritate. He himself first presented the distorted image of a wild Irish boy who
arrived wide-eyed and ignorant in London. (His
enemies merely helped to perpetuate it.) He himself
was responsible for the caricatured pseudo-French,
pseudo-English figure that later returned to Ireland.
But Moore's susceptibility to influences, his willingness
to clothe himself in the expectations of others, was
always more than role playing for the sake of remaining stage center. His "nature like a smooth sheet of
wax" provided his artistic self with endless opportuni-
ties for imaginative experimentation. Throughout his
life he was always his own best work of art.

Born of the fourth generation to live in Moore Hall,
County Mayo, George Moore belonged to a family that
claimed descent from Sir Thomas More, author of
Utopia. In the eighteenth century, when anti-Catholic
laws restricted education in Ireland and drove many
Catholic Irishmen abroad, his great-uncles had been
sent to fine continental schools and his great-grand-
father had been received at the Spanish court. His
grandfather, a historian, author of *History of the British
Revolution of 1688* and *A Treatise on the Art of
Reasoning*, moved easily in London intellectual circles
of the early nineteenth century. George Henry Moore,
the novelist's father, began his writing career at the
age of seventeen with a long Byronic poem, "Irene,"
which was published in the *London and Dublin Magazine*. Later, as a member of Parliament, he earned a
reputation for eloquence in both England and Ireland.

"Literature so accumulated at Moore Hall during his lifetime," according to Joseph Hone, "that George [Henry] Moore's library had eventually to be extended so as to take in all the guest rooms at the back of the house on the ground floor." Millais was his friend; Landseer was an esteemed acquaintance; other prominent artists, writers, and political figures visited him in London and Mayo.

Clearly, the background of George Moore, novelist, was not the cultural desert he later led others to believe. W. B. Yeats, for example, thought he had come from "a house where there was no culture as Symons and I understand the word," and Frank Harris repeated a conversation with Moore in which the latter reportedly declared that Shakespeare, the Bible, and English and world classics were unfamiliar to him. But his grandfather and father had been very much a part of the social and intellectual life of their day, and Moore Hall, in which the novelist was brought up, reflected their social position and cultural and intellectual interests.

George Augustus Moore, as the novelist was christened, was born in the house overlooking Lough Carra on February 24, 1852. From the first he was apparently a difficult child. He was backward in talking; later, he showed a similar recalcitrance in learning to read and write. His early education was shared at home with a second child, Maurice, under an English governess, Miss Westby. His parents helped acquaint him with fiction, poetry, and travel literature through the stories they told: Mrs. Moore, the former Mary Blake, used to recite whole passages from Sir Walter Scott's novels by heart; George Henry narrated tales partly drawn from his own readings, partly from his experiences in the East. Artists and writers who traveled west from London and Dublin were entertained at Moore Hall. The Wilde boys, Oscar and Willie, who summered at Cong with their father, were occasional afternoon visitors. When George was five, his father temporarily lost his seat in Parliament and, returning to the interests of his youth, began to build up racing stables at Moore Hall. By 1861, the election debts had been paid, largely by the winnings of a colt named Croaghpatrick, and George was sent to the school where, as a boy, his father had distinguished himself.

George Moore's experiences at St. Mary's, in Oscott, near Birmingham, however, bore no resemblance to those of his father. He was not academically inclined, nor had he any interest in becoming so. A period of poor health relieved him, in 1863, of the necessity of remaining at Oscott for a time; rejoicing in his good luck, he spent his days among his father's stable boys and his nights dreaming of becoming a jockey. In 1865, however, he was sent back to school, where the headmaster, J. Spencer Northcote, a former Anglican from Oxford who had come under the influence of Newman, despaired of ever being able to educate him. Declaring him "deplorably deficient," he added in a letter to George Henry Moore (quoted by Hone, *The Moores of Moore Hall,* p. 174), "it is by no means easy to see how his deficits are to be supplied." A few years later, Northcote was relieved of the responsibility. Young

George was withdrawn from Oscott at the age of sixteen and was returned for a brief period to the Mayo countryside he loved. In one of his autobiographical accounts, Moore writes that the reason for his withdrawal from school was an intrigue with a housemaid, whom he offered to marry; his brother, however, recollects no such scandal, and letters from the school indicate that poor scholarship and a refusal to go to confession were more likely the cause. Whatever truth there might have been to George's account, if any, possibly was occasioned by his interest in Shelley's life and works. If Shelley's involvement with Harriet had ended his formal education, Moore, a reluctant scholar with a taste for the dramatic, well might have tried—or later wished that he had tried—the same.

Departure from Oscott, in any case, marked the end of George's formal schooling, but by no means did it terminate his education. He had been at St. Mary's a total of five years, and he had been admitted after several years of lessons from Miss Westby. Stories later circulated concerning his unfamiliarity with literature and the arts cannot be credited in the face of these facts. Even a failing student at Oscott would have had more cultural training than they imply. In addition, a tutor, Father James, was called to Moore Hall to help George continue his studies in the classics. Together they read first Caesar and then Propertius, until George repeated his tutor's prediction that he would develop genuine ability in classical studies. His mother laughed; Moore laughed, too—Byronically— and dropped Latin. Meanwhile he spent long hours

exploring his father's library. Bored by Scott, despite
his mother's attempt to engage him on picnics by
reciting passages from *Marmion* and his father's insistence on reading aloud *The Lay of the Last Min-
strel,* he read the poetry of Cowley, Coleridge, and
Byron, which was more to his taste, plus Burke's
speeches, which his father had recommended to him.
By the time he was twenty-one, Moore declared in his
introduction to *An Anthology of Pure Poetry* that he
had read most of the English poets. Although else-
where he poses as a noble savage or Wordsworthian
child in his youth, his easy references to poets and
poetry lends credence to the statement, with allowance
for the hyperbole of *most.*

Shortly after Moore left Oscott, his father once again
was elected to represent Mayo in Parliament. Moore
Hall was closed, and the family was removed to South
Kensington, London, close to the art schools and gal-
leries where young George first became acquainted
with the world of painting and painters. In London,
according to John Freeman, Moore read such books
as *Middlemarch,* Kant's *Critique of Pure Reason,* and
a history of civilization. He also showed considerable
interest in the life of his grandfather, and he sometimes spoke of a book written about another man
similarly admired by his heirs: *A Russian Gentleman,
Years of Childhood,* by Aksakoff.

In view of these facts, it seems clear, as Malcolm
Brown has pointed out, that "much of Moore's claim
to ignorance was plain hoax. . . . He did know a re-
spectably wide range of literature, and what he knew

he knew extraordinarily well." His formal education was admittedly limited, but his cultural background and intellectual milieu equipped him to enter English society with as much ease and assurance as is common to sensitive young men from well-to-do families. After his father's death in 1870, Moore continued to live for a time in South Kensington with his family, where together he and his brother Maurice read and discussed Dickens, history, and philosophy. That their training was far from inadequate seems evident from the fact that all the Moore boys later distinguished themselves in letters: after his retirement from the army, Maurice edited the literary remains of his father and grandfather and wrote a biography of his father; Augustus earned a living on Fleet Street, writing opera librettos and contributing to humor journals; Julian, the serious scholar among the four, a book collector with a unique knowledge of book bindings, devoted many years to tracing the origins of the legend of Tristan and Isolde.

Moore's insistence on his own lack of knowledge was surely more philosophical than real. That men are cursed with instinctive bad taste that needs education was frequently one of his contentions. Titian and Holbein, he confessed, had meant but little to him in his youth. He had to pass through "many stages of comprehension," he avowed, before he could distinguish reasons for greatness in art. Nevertheless, Moore's testimony indicates that in his youth he was acquainted with paintings by Titian and Holbein, a fact that clearly contradicts Yeats's statement that Moore came from a home of "no culture." The fact is that Moore was a man of sufficient culture to distinguish between acquaintance and knowledge; for him, a high degree of comprehension was essential to the latter. He passed his "stages of comprehension" chiefly through his study of painting, beginning as a classicist, adopting aesthetic theories that reached back to the eighteenth century, discarding them one by one as he was introduced to and influenced by later theories of art. In the end, although he himself gave up all hope of becoming a painter, he had acquired sufficient knowledge of history and technique to be regarded as an astute essayist on contemporary art.

2

An Apprenticeship in Art

As the record of George Moore's education extends long after his formal schooling had ended, so the story of his training as an artist begins many years before he entered drawing classes in South Kensington, England. In a sense, it starts, perhaps, with his impressions of Muckloon, Lough Carra, and the Mayo countryside in which he was born. Here the sky overhead is often gray with undulant clouds through which filter light rays of varying intensity. These give to the air a luminosity that is reflected in the multiple shades of green for which the Irish landscape is famous. The lake itself mirrors the sky, changing as it changes, from light to dark and back to light again. In the distance, the Partry mountains are blue against the brighter horizon; the nearer shadows of the copsewood are of deeper intensity. Even today, it is difficult to stand on the hill, next to the burnt-out shell of Moore Hall, and not think first of Corot, next of a Turner sky, and finally, catching a glimpse of figures in the distance, of a Greek frieze, or perhaps of some medieval tapestry. Occasionally, a ray of sunshine breaks through the clouds. Then the far landscape appears to have been touched by the brush of Renoir or Manet, and the nearer scene glows like the gardens of Berthe Morisot.

All the young Moores who grew up on the hill in Mayo explored picturesque Carra Castle at the end of the lake; historic Ballintubber, Cathal Crovedearg O'Conor's ancient abbey, then unroofed; and the natural world of the small island to which Marban, a hermit, had withdrawn centuries ago. Servants told them stories about the place, throwing over it that "certain colouring of imagination, whereby ordinary things should be presented to the mind in an unusual aspect," from which Wordsworth had created poetry. It was a home to nourish a romantic temperament.

George Henry Moore, however, had had an eighteenth-century upbringing. He had been taught the aesthetic theories of Reynolds and the Royal Society; he had learned to appreciate painting in the grand manner. Inside, Moore Hall was decorated according to his preferences. Sculptured figures of mermen and mermaids supported an intricately carved mantelpiece in the oak-paneled dining room. Decorations in the drawing room expressed an admiration for Greek classical civilization. (Taken from sketches George Henry Moore had made during a trip to the East, later they were borrowed by his son for the decorations of Mrs. Bentham's ballroom in *A Modern Lover* and *Lewis Seymour and Some Women*.) In painting, he favored large historical canvasses and classical scenes, but he had a weakness, too, for pictures of racehorses, and these shared wall space with the gilt-framed portraits that had been handed down in the family for generations.

Art, for George Henry Moore, was not a profession but an accomplishment. It was his responsibility, he believed, to develop sound artistic judgment in his growing sons. In London, in the short years between his eldest son's departure from Oscott and his death, he often visited the National Gallery with young George and Maurice. There he tried to draw the attention of the two boys to technique, pointing out how the artist achieved a desired effect through some device such as the foreshortening of an arm. Young George's attention wandered, however, to other Venuses. During these London years, if Edward Dayne of *Confessions of a Young Man* (1888) reflects his tastes, it was a Botticelli that held him "in tether."

It was through his father, however, that young George first met Jim Browne, the great blond painter of historical canvases and classical narratives whom he idolized and imitated until, in Paris in 1874, a new idol displaced him. Browne, a distant kinsman, was the artist of "The Burial of an Indian Chief," a large painting which hung over the stairwell at Moore Hall. One of his works had been accepted by the Royal Academy. As depicted in *Confessions of a Young Man,* he "talked incessantly about beautiful women," and painted them "sometimes larger than life, in somnolent attitudes." Browne's conversation as much as his painting fascinated the young man, and when he later told

Moore that France was the only place to study art, there was no question but that the trip someday had to be made.

While his father lived, however, George Moore seemed destined for a military career. He attended art classes at the South Kensington Museum at night, but by day he was supposed to be studying with his tutor, Jurles, for the army examinations. Actually, when he was not in the betting circles at St. John's Wood, he was pursuing his new interest, visiting museums and art collectors on his own. During his early London years, Hone reports in the biography, Moore sometimes stood outside a Kensington house in which he knew there was a collection of "moderns" until the owner went out. Then he knocked at the door and bribed the servants to allow him to see a famous Rossetti.

Moore arrived at his taste for the Pre-Raphaelites independently; it was not fostered by his father. To be sure, Millais, a member of the Brotherhood, was his father's friend, but George Henry Moore was, in general, lukewarm to the style popularized by Rossetti and his followers. The Pre-Raphaelites were called "moderns" because they were the rebels, painting in opposition to the established, dominant Academy; George Henry Moore was an admirer of antiquities. But by 1870 the rebellion of the Pre-Raphaelites was old, and they seemed far less radical than they had in 1848 when the Brotherhood was founded. In addition, John Ruskin had taken them under his protection, making them respectable. If George Henry Moore could not support the Pre-Raphaelites, at least he did not oppose them.

George Henry Moore's death in 1870 was both blow and blessing to George Moore. On the one hand, it freed him from the necessity of pretending to continue his studies for the army examinations; on the other hand, if *Confessions of a Young Man* can be believed, it took from him "the one pure image of his mind, the one true affection." Meanwhile, his desire to become an artist had been strengthened by his London experiences: "This future self, this ideal George Moore, beckoned me, lured like a ghost . . . the self on whose creation I was enthusiastically determined." His mother, however, dissuaded him from leaving for Paris until he was of age.

Attitudes toward art in nineteenth-century England, especially at the time of George Henry Moore's death, were directed in large part by the writings of John Ruskin. A Victorian by upbringing and a classicist in his concern for order, Ruskin was also, paradoxically, a naturalist and an associationalist. His aesthetic theories, shaped by preconceived moral opinions, were highly structured, with categories and qualities carefully defined as Baconian "Ideas" and "Provinces." At bottom, however, they were founded upon emotional perception. And Ruskin's concept of the artist did much to liberate England from neoclassical prejudices. The artist's function, according to Ruskin's description in *Stones of Venice,* was to be "a seeing and feeling creature, to be an instrument of such tenderness and sensitiveness, that no shadow, no hue, no line, no

instantaneous and evanescent expression of the visible
things around him, nor any of the emotions which they
are capable of conveying to the spirit which has been
given him, shall either be left unrecorded, or fade
from the book of record. . . . The work of his life is
to be two-fold only; to see, to feel."

In conversation with William Archer, Moore stated
that he had never read Ruskin, but acknowledged that
they both had said much that was similar about art
and perception. Given Moore's tendency to absorb
his environment and Ruskin's position in the English
art world of 1870 to 1875, it would be curious if such
similarities were not found. At the same time, the
Royal Academy, ruled by more conservative opinion,
regarded Greek art as the supreme achievement and
Greek antiquities as proper models for aspiring art
students, and George Moore responded to it as well.
He learned to draw parts of the body (hands especially
fascinated him), he learned about symmetry and balance of elements, and he learned to sketch or outline
a picture before he began to paint it. Then he set out
for France, where different theories prevailed and
different techniques were practiced, and where a different George Moore emerged, the stable part of his
nature always having been, as Humbert Wolfe observed, his tendency "to reflect rather than to mould
the world of the moment."

George Moore arrived in Paris at six-thirty in the
morning on March 13, 1873. He had turned twenty-
one just a few weeks before, on February 24. His first
impression of the city, as recalled in *Confessions of a*

Young Man, were not favorable: Paris was a "tall, haggard city." Aside from the "pale, sloppy, yellow houses," there was "an oppressive absence of colour; a peculiar bleakness in the streets." His first task, dramatized in *Confessions of a Young Man,* was to find a teacher: "Day after day I walked up and down the Boulevards, studying the photographs of the salon pictures, trying to find a painter to whom I might address myself with confidence." Alexandre Cabanel was the first to be approached: the two paintings that attracted Moore to him, significantly, were a classical scene (a satyr breaking through branches, a woman in his arms) and a Renaissance portrait (Dante reading before a frightened audience). Cabanel recommended study at the Beaux Arts, where he was a professor; Moore committed himself to a schedule more rigorous than any he had experienced before. No doubt Hone and Collet are correct in attributing Moore's rapid withdrawal from the Beaux Arts to early hours and hard work: by his own admission, at twenty-one, he was a young man *"qui tenait à ses aises."* But Moore also was self-conscious and full of self-doubt; very likely open comparison of his work with that of other students made him uncomfortable in the public atmosphere of the studio. In any case, he next sought private lessons, then enrolled at the Salon Julien where he hoped to learn how to paint indolent nudes with long hair, slender hips, and delicate hands after the manner of Jules Lefebvre, who instructed there.

Of himself during these first months in Paris, Moore

has said, "I was a childish boy of one-and-twenty who knew nothing, and to whom the world was astonishingly new." His own estimate of his naïveté is supported by two facts: first, although he had planned the trip for three years, he had little working knowledge of the French language when he arrived; second, although he had come to France to learn art as it was not taught in England, the first masters he approached were those who painted familiar subjects in a familiar manner. There were differences in technique, however, which soon became apparent to George Moore. While in English studios pupils were taught to outline figures, in French ateliers they constructed the human body using dioramic shapes, some light, some shadowed. For George Moore, who always responded to new ways of seeing the visible world, the French system—and it was a system, which also contributed to its appeal—was a revelation. In a letter to his mother, quoted by Hone, Moore declared that Cabanel had taught him to draw. In comparison with the teachers he had had in London, Cabanel, Lefebvre, Girôme, and Meissonier were "trained artists."

In the years between 1873 and 1880, Moore passed an apprenticeship in French art and French society, moving gradually from the Salon Julien to the cafés of Montmartre and finally to the balls and dinner parties where he became an accepted member of *le beau monde*. He was soon acquainted with the leaders of both the world of art and the world of fashion; under their tutelage, he studied trends and techniques in both life and painting that carried him far beyond what once had appeared to him to be fashion and talent in Jim Browne's London studio. For a brief period, in 1874, Moore returned to London, taking a studio in Cromwell Mews, where he painted women in the style of Rossetti and chatted with his father's old friend, Millais, who sometimes visited him. He also attended Barthe's classes, where he met Whistler, whom he later, grudgingly, came to admire. But for the most part, these years belonged to France.

The story of his French years has been told and retold by Moore in his autobiographical writings. In large part, however, these accounts cannot be taken literally, as Hone has warned, since "Moore wrote into the memories of his early days in Paris much that he acquired on later visits." Moreover, Moore never could resist the temptation to fictionalize himself and his experiences, to remake life "artistically" in conversations and private letters as well as in so-called autobiographical sketches intended for his public. Moore's portrait of himself may owe one debt, for example, to Des Esseintes, the hero of Huysmans's *A Rebours,* and another to d'Albert, of Gautier's *Mademoiselle de Maupin.* And to models drawn from literature, he added real ones, such as Lewis Hawkins (Lewis Ponsonby Marshall of *Confessions of a Young Man* and *Hail and Farewell*) .

A naturalized Frenchman, born in Stuttgart, brought up in Brussels, Hawkins first introduced himself to Moore as a cousin of Moore's London idol, Jim Browne —whom he immediately replaced. He had, wrote Moore, beautiful broad shoulders, a long neck, tiny

hands, a narrow face, and eyes "full of intelligence
and fascination." He was a cosmopolitan: Paris was,
to him, an intimate acquaintance, and he spoke famil-
iarly—in excellent English—of other European capitals
as well. He also had a shallow talent and easy versa-
tility that seemed deep and genuine to the naïve young
Irishman. At the Salon Julien he sketched with facility;
in his baroque apartment, to which he invited Moore,
he played a waltz of his own composition—a trifle, he
announced, which he had tossed off in a passing mood.
It seemed to Moore that Hawkins had a beautiful
talent, beautiful manners, beautiful clothes, a beautiful
apartment, and a beautiful mistress. There seemed no
better way to learn the ways of the fashionable French
world than to imitate him: "I used him without shame
or stint," admits Moore, through the character-narrator of *Confessions of a Young Man,* "as I have used
all those with whom I have been brought into close
contact."

Despite his cosmopolitan background and exotic
tastes in furnishings, Hawkins apparently was as conservative as Moore in his approach to art. Julien's
studio was not avant-garde. Its teachers emphasized
draftsmanship; the works produced there, by staff
and students alike, were semiclassical and objective,
not unlike those of Couture's studio, where Manet
first studied art. In 1875, at the Hotel Drouot, an auction of impressionist paintings was held. Hawkins and
Moore were among the students who went to sneer at
the work of Monet, Sisley, Renoir, and Berthe Morisot.
As described in *Confessions of a Young Man,* they

were "insolent with patent leather shoes and bright kid gloves and armed with all the jargon of the school. *'Cette jambe ne porte pas;' 'La nature ne se fait pas comme ça;' 'on dessine par les masses; combien de têtes?' 'Sept et demi.'* "

The reaction of Julien's students to the work of the impressionists was later repeated in literature by the reaction of readers to aesthetic novels. E. M. Forster has described the problem in *Aspects of the Novel:* "All novels contain tables and chairs, and most readers of fiction look for them first." The novelist, however, often has a different point of view. "He is not looking at the tables and chairs at all, and that is why they are out of focus. We only see what he does not focus— not what he does—and in our blindness we laugh at him." By the time Moore revised *Confessions of a Young Man* for the 1916 edition, his artistic vision, including hindsight, had improved. Of the 1875 auction, he wrote belatedly, "deep down in our souls we knew that we were lying—at least I did."

Moore stopped laughing at impressionism, actually, after he had joined the circle at the Nouvelles Athènes. By 1876, he had begun to doubt the kind of art that he was engaged in, to regard "the delineation of a nymph, or youth bathing . . . as a very narrow channel to carry off the strong, full tide of a man's thought." Before long, he doubted as well his own abilities as an artist. Meanwhile, Bernard Lopez (Duval of *Confessions of a Young Man*), a playwright who had, in better days, collaborated with some of the great names of French literature, had introduced Moore to Montmartre café society. First he met Villiers de l'Isle Adam; this meeting led to an introduction to Mallarmé; through Mallarmé, Moore met Manet, who invited him to his studio in the rue St. Petersbourg. In Manet's studio and the Montmartre cafés where impressionist painters, naturalistic novelists, and Parnassian poets gathered, Moore also met Degas, Daudet, Renoir, Sisley, Monet, Pissarro, Zola, Edmond Goncourt, and Turgenev. The artists of this group were of central importance; except for those named above, the writers were generally doubtful of their own ability and envied that of the painter.

Moore, who was then caught between art and literature—he was trying his hand at decadent verse, he had completed one play, and he would shortly collaborate with Lopez on another—watched and listened. Perhaps, if he could not paint pictures, he could write about them. Gautier, a painter who had become first a poet and then a novelist, was helping to form the taste of a new generation through his guidebooks and other essays on art. Baudelaire's salon reviews had attracted attention and carried weight. Zola often reviewed the work of artists in his newspaper articles. Moore considered that he might do the same. The man who seemed most worthy of his attention, the one whose work he found most provocative, was Edouard Manet, an artist whose background and temperament were similar to Moore's.

By 1877, when Moore probably became a regular visitor at his studio, Manet had established a reputation as a leader of a new art movement in France. An early rebel against the pale classicism and artificial narration of traditional art as it was then practiced, Manet had experimented with the styles of Hals, Rembrandt, Titian, Tintoretto, Velasquez, and Goya before finding his own style, first apparent in *Le Déjeuner sur l'herbe*. Substituting for traditional chiaroscuro bright colors through which he achieved perspective by the use of tone rather than light and shadow, Manet had opened the door to impressionism. Moreover, instead of choosing models proportioned according to neoclassical ideals, painted nude or draped in the costumes of antiquity, Manet placed middle-class men in middle-class clothing on his canvas. Thus he and his followers were automatically aligned with the naturalists in literature.

A second member of the Montmartre group who taught George Moore new ways in which, in the words of Gautier, "the visible world was visible" was Degas. A pupil of Ingres, a classicist whom Moore continued to admire long after he became an apostle of impressionism, Degas had learned from his master that acuteness of drawing discerned by Moore in his treatment of the "humblest aspects of modern life." Unlike other French artists who had developed under the neoclassicists, Degas did not draw by masses, Moore noted, but by character. He was, therefore, another innovator of the time, although less recognized as such—partly as a result of his own reticence and insistence upon privacy.

These were the two men whose theories of art proved significant in the development of George Moore's aesthetic. Although they could not teach him art, as John Freeman has observed, "he did learn to look with their eyes and to weigh with their measure."

3
The Making of a Novelist

In an anecdote frequently quoted from *Confessions of a Young Man,* George Moore revealed what he considered to be the earliest awakening of his interest in literature. It was through an incident of the kind which James Joyce later called an *epiphany:* a name mentioned in casual conversation permeated the consciousness of a sleepy eleven-year-old boy who, a moment past, had been half-concentrating his visual attention on a flock of birds rising from an Irish bog to form a pattern against distant blue mountains. Scene and name fused to become the outward manifestation of an inward experience that had, for the boy, mystical connotations. At the first opportunity, he searched his father's library for the novel to which the name belonged in a Proustian attempt to recapture the sensations of that moment. He read the book—*Lady Audley's Secret* by Mary Elizabeth Braddon—"eagerly, passionately, vehemently." Thereafter, he devoured every other book by Miss Braddon that he could obtain, finding in them an experiential

perception of beauty that depended as much on his own
excited expectation as on Miss Braddon's melodramatic
prose. Moore revised his account of the incident in his
introduction to *An Anthology of Pure Poetry:* in the
later version memory seems somewhat blurred. He was
a child of nine, ten, or eleven, he says (an impossibility,
since *Lady Audley's Secret* was not published until he
was eleven), and the family coach was taking him, his
brother, and his parents to Headfort, not home from
Oscott, as Joseph Hone suggests. The hypnotic effect was
caused not by birds and mountains, but by the swinging
of the coach and the shining of the sun on his face. At
this writing, Moore also recalls *Lady Audley's Secret*
inaccurately, referring to it as "the story of a woman who
ran away with her groom," which it is not. What remains, however, despite the fading of the facts, is the
recollection of emotional impact. Unlike many other
dramatic incidents recalled by George Moore, its ac-
curacy has not been challenged by his brother, Colonel
Maurice Moore, whose imagination, according to
Joseph Hone, was less apt to color the events of their
childhood.

In *A Doctor's Wife,* an adaptation by Miss Braddon
of Flaubert's *Madame Bovary,* Moore found inspiration
for still another epiphany: the heroine read not romantic novels, but romantic poetry—the poetry of Shelley
and Byron. It was the name *Shelley* that seemed to him,
this time, to have a magical quality. The epiphany—or
echo-augury, as George Moore later called such experiences—depended for him as for Joyce on a pattern
of events, feelings, or perceptions: one event, feeling,

or perception might be the trigger, but only in association with others. Thus Shelley's name apparently was read without unusual effect in *Lady Audley's Secret,* where he was listed as one of the favorite poets of the "sentimental young woman" to whom George Talboys recounts the first part of his story; it struck Moore's youthful imagination only when he encountered it in the later book. But once a word or scene was infused with mystical meaning, it never quite returned to the commonplace, according to Moore. So Coleridge's "Christabel," quoted by father to son in an intimate moment when George Moore was watching his father shaving, never lost its beauty; the appeal of the lines was "increased . . . by association with the moment" when they were heard for the first time.

The library at Moore Hall contained a volume of Shelley's poetry. "Henceforth," wrote Moore, "the little volume never left my pocket, and I read the dazzling stanzas by the shores of a pale Irish lake. . . ." The poem to which he immediately responded, in which he immediately saw himself, was appropriately entitled "The Sensitive Plant." In a lifetime of changing loyalties, it continued to fascinate him, even in old age, when he could still recall its lines with pleasure.

Poetry was the literary genre in which George Moore first was published when finally he relinquished all hope of a painting career. His model, however, was not Shelley but Baudelaire. His slim volume of Baudelairean bad verse, *Flowers of Passion,* which appeared in 1878, quickly drew severe criticism from those who noticed it at all. Earlier, according to Joseph Hone,

Moore had suffered another literary failure: *Worldli-ness,* a comedy in three acts, published in London in 1874. Hone marks the date with a question mark and does not include the name of the publisher: what information exists about the play is sketchy at best. The title is included in a bibliography by I. A. Williams, first printed in 1921; it is not repeated in Henry Danielson's bibliography appended to John Freeman's *Portrait.* Edward Gilcher, who reports that the *London Mercury* of October, 1921, failed to turn up a copy despite an offer of a £100 reward, questions whether or not the play ever was published at all. Gilcher's correspondence with Allan Wade, however, suggests that *Worldliness* might have been printed in a small limited edition for circulation to theater managers, in which case the copies probably were quickly discarded by those who received them. In any case, no trace of *Worldliness* remains today.

Characteristically undiscouraged, in any case, although he had failed to attract favorable attention as a poet, Moore decided to try the theater managers again. His next effort was a tragedy (*Martin Luther,* 1879) in which he had the assistance of Bernard Lopez, described on the title page as the collaborator of "Scribe, Méry, Auguste Lefranc, Théophile Gautier, Alexandre Dumas père, Victor Séjour, Alboize, Charles Desnoyer, Gérard de Nerval, Dupenty, Laurencin, Grangé, Hippolyte Cogniard, Lelarge, Delacour, Varin, Charles Narrey, Rochefort père, Dumanoir, Clairville et Saint-Georges." The list was impressive but the play was not. It was never produced, and its chief interest today is its preface, which, according to Ernest Boyd (*Portraits: Real and Imaginary*, London, 1924), "may be cited as the authentic precursor of the prefaces subsequently made famous by Bernard Shaw."

Still undiscouraged as a writer, even by lack of interest in *Martin Luther*, Moore returned to poetry again. *Pagan Poems* (1881) was partly a new work, partly a borrowing from its unsuccessful predecessor. If it did not establish Moore's fame, at least it created for him some kind of reputation in London. *Pagan* was the name by which it became known, not always kindly, but Moore was pleased with any recognition of his work: happily he adopted the sobriquet for occasional use as a pen name. No more volumes of poetry appeared, although Moore's verse continued to find space in newspapers and journals from time to time. And never able to give up entirely, Moore often reprinted lines from his early work in later novels, essays, and tales.

Meanwhile, Moore had moved from Paris to London. Diminished rent receipts from Moore Hall had cut his income and left him in debt to his uncle, Joseph Blake of Ballinafad, who had been acting as his agent. After the first shock of finding himself no longer a member of the leisure class, Moore set about trying to manage his affairs more efficiently. His first step was to ask young Tom Ruttledge, a neighbor, to take over the accounts that Blake refused to continue handling; next he inspected his properties, noted his assets and liabilities, raised enough by mortgage to pay his debt to his uncle, and sold timber from the woods around

Moore Hall to establish a small cash reserve for himself. Then he returned to London to see if he could earn a living, as he hoped, by his pen. Like his father, he had refrained from evicting any of his tenants to improve his own financial situation, despite the fact that many—encouraged by the Land League and other tenants' rights groups—had refused to pay rent. And although he insisted that he could never settle down to permanent residence at Moore Hall and pretended disinterest in the problems besetting the countryside, it is clear from Moore's later writings that, as Hone states, "he kept his eyes and ears open" and formed opinions that later proved to be not only educated but well researched.

In London before his extended business trip to Mayo, Moore had had a job for a short time—he was second secretary for two guineas a week on the *Examiner,* and "dear at the price," Hone reports (*Life of George Moore,* p. 83), quoting Heinrich Felbermann, editor and proprietor of the paper. On his return he worked on a novel (later abandoned, if the account in *Confessions of a Young Man* is accurate) and collaborated with his brother, Augustus, on a translation of Louis Clairville's lyrics for *Les Cloches de Corneville,* a comic opera by Robert Planquette. At long last something by Moore actually was performed before a live audience, if only for a brief run: *Cloches* was produced in London in the spring of 1883. By early summer the thirty-one-year-old author also had a novel in print, *A Modern Lover,* published by Tinsley. A few short stories and several reviews and short articles, the latter two chiefly unsigned, also appeared between 1880 and 1883. Moore had begun to establish a reputation for serious literary work.

The central figure of *A Modern Lover* is an artist, Lewis Seymour, whose gradual climb to fame, wealth, and social position is accomplished principally at the expense of three women. The first is a poor girl, Gwynnie Lloyd. She divests herself of both honor and clothing to pose nude for Seymour. Unable to face him again, yet still in love with him, she runs away from the cheap lodging house where they have been fellow roomers. The second, Lucy Bentham, is an older but still attractive woman of means. Separated from her husband, she develops a maternal interest in the struggling artist, engages him to decorate her ballroom, underwrites his training in Paris, becomes his mistress, subsidizes his work, selflessly helps him arrange a good match, and believes in him to the very end. The third, Lady Helen, is a beautiful but willful young lady of high social position. Pushing aside other worthy contenders for her hand, she determines, despite parental opposition, to become Seymour's bride, only to find in him a shallow talent and a weak philandering nature. Nevertheless, having chosen her lot, Lady Helen uses her beauty, strength of character, and social position to further her husband's career. She succeeds in forcing his election to the Royal Academy, an honor which he does not deserve and could not have won on his own. At the moment of supreme triumph, there is also supreme disillusion. Her maid, previously unrecognized because she has been disfigured by smallpox, is revealed as

Gwynnie Lloyd. When Gwynnie sobs out her story, both she and Lady Helen realize how much they have paid for Seymour's success. Mrs. Bentham, however, remains certain that he has deserved it. Similarities to Maupassant's *Bel Ami* have been noted; the French story, however (as Hone, Brown, and others have also pointed out), was published after *A Modern Lover* and was therefore not its source.

Like the figures of early Italian painting, all the characters of *A Modern Lover* are described in detail. There is no perspective; there are no half-delineated supporting characters in the background. Although she is but a minor character, for example, Mrs. Thorpe, Mrs. Bentham's elderly companion, is as painstakingly portrayed—in person, dress, mannerism, and response— as Mrs. Bentham herself. Settings are similarly treated, whether or not they contribute to mood or character.

Structurally, the novel reveals a classical balance of elements: Gwynnie Lloyd's story is told in the opening pages; it is retold at the conclusion. In each volume, a discussion of the conflict between opposing schools of art interrupts the narrative at midpoint. In the first three chapters of volume one, Gwynnie passes out of Lewis's life. In the final three chapters of volume one, Lady Helen enters it. Volume two begins with Lewis leaving Mrs. Bentham to go to Paris. They are re-united; the volume ends with his leaving Mrs. Bentham to go to Lady Helen. In the opening pages of volume three, Gwynnie collapses when she hears whom her mistress is to marry; in the closing pages, she again collapses when her past is brought to light.

Other techniques probably derived from Moore's early art background are apparent in character delineation and in certain settings described in the novel. Mr. Bendish and Lewis in Bendish's gallery present a contrast in romantic, picturesque portraiture on the one hand and classical, academic portraiture on the other. "The last speaker was an old, wizened little creature, with a grizzled white beard; the other was a young man of exquisite beauty, his feminine grace seemed like a relic of ancient Greece. . . ." Mrs. Bentham's ballroom is inspired by classical art: the cornices and moldings seem to be of white marble (actually, they had been modeled from plaster of Paris following Greek examples). Mrs. Bentham asks Lewis to choose designs for the panels from seventeenth-century engravings of the kind approved by Moore's father. There are "Venuses and Cupids to no end; flowers, tendrils, grapes, all kinds of fruit in profusion." The artists represented are Boucher, Watteau, and others admired by the academicians. Mrs. Bentham's favorite panel, when the work is completed, is typical of the whole: it depicts a nymph seated high on a bower made of tendrils and roses, surrounded by a ring of cupids who dance to the music she plays on her reed flute.

A biographical anecdote about a neoclassic painter—Ingres, and his *La Source*—may have been the germ of Gwynnie Lloyd's sacrifice. "What care I," asks Moore in *Confessions of a Young Man,* "that the virtue of some sixteen-year-old maiden was the price . . . ?" Gwynnie's reputation, if not her virtue, is the price of Lewis's painting. (The price is also paid by the young model of "In the Clay," a short story about a sculptor in a later work, *The Untilled Field*.) Gwynnie herself is a poor working girl, of the type painted in squalid surroundings by such artists as Degas, Millet, and Clausen. Lewis, however (the possibility of irony is not remote), finds in her a perfect model for a painting of Venus rising from the sea, tossing a cloud of hair about her body—an obvious imitation of the Botticelli that Moore had admired in the National Gallery. Lady Helen, too, has a classical beauty: like a statue, she is immaculately white, "the type of all that is elegant," yet with a certain hardness or coldness. Speaking of her, two minor characters, Day and Ripple, describe her as being "very Greek" in appearance. Mrs. Bentham seems more an individual, less a type. But both Lady Helen and Mrs. Bentham have the abundant hair and large bosom found in paintings by the Pre-Raphaelites and Whistler. (Moore himself, for a short while, had a studio in Cromwell Mews, where he painted Rossetti-like portraits of women.) Lady Helen and Mrs. Bentham are also tall; as John Freeman points out, Jim Browne had taught Moore to admire tall women with abundant bosoms as subjects for painting as well as for romance.

Lewis Seymour has generally been regarded as a fictional portrait of Lewis Weldon Hawkins, whom Moore knew in Paris. Moore himself has admitted that he studied Hawkins carefully: "my friend became to me . . . a subject for dissection; the general attitude of his mind and its various turns, all the apparent contradictions, and how they could be explained, classified, and reduced to one primary law, were to me a constant source of thought." To be sure, Lewis Seymour's syco- phantic behavior is in agreement with what Moore tells of Hawkins in his autobiographies. And Lewis Seymour has "large, tender blue eyes" so "full of intelligence and fascination," like the eyes of Hawkins, but his hips are broad and his shoulders are narrow and sloping —like those of George Moore. Seymour, in fact, has a background which includes as many points of similarity to Moore's life as to that of Hawkins. Like his author, he has an intelligence that dawned slowly: not until he was over fifteen did his mind begin to brighten. Moore had once felt that applause of his drawings in a small, South Kensington circle augured wider success; Seymour "thought that because he had succeeded in the country, he would succeed in the big city." Both young Moore and young Seymour at first knew nothing of the contemporary art world; Seymour had seen "nothing but the plaster casts in the training school, the pictures in the country houses he visited, and small photographs of a new school, which, in a kind of early Italian form, gave expression to much ephemeral lan- gour. This Lewis thought the *beau ideal* of all that life could desire. . . ."

Similar to Moore's struggle to realize himself as an artist, as described in his autobiographical writings, are the occasional anguished attempts of Lewis Seymour:

Again he fell a victim to that most terrible of maladies, the love of art for art; again he suffered the pain of the imperious want to translate his thoughts, his visions, his dreams; again he felt come over him the terrible shuddering of art, the emotion of the subject found, of the scene which became clear. He suffered all the pain of this terrible child-bearing without the supreme happiness of deliverance. His pains were infinite but fruitless, for the impalpable something which tempted, tortured him, faded into nothing when he attempted to reduce the unapparent reality into pictures.

The salon in which Seymour studies during his first months in Paris is identified as the Beaux Arts, which Moore left after a few days. In descriptive detail, however, it resembles more closely the Salon Julien, with which Moore was better acquainted.

Seymour's caddish behavior has its counterpart in Moore's fantasies, reported by Charles Morgan: George Bernard Shaw, for example, recalled that Moore was always telling stories about himself and women in rooms full of mirrors and chandeliers; the stories usually ended with the women throwing lamps at him, driving him from the house. Challenged concerning the truth of such stories, Moore brushed aside interruptions, without anger, but with determination to continue his tale to the end.

The extent to which Lewis Seymour is a self-portrait of George Moore is the extent to which Moore had once modeled himself on such men as Jim Browne and Lewis Weldon Hawkins; it is therefore a limited portrait, restricted to the period between Moore's decision to become an artist and his introduction to the Nouvelle Athènes. Seymour's opinions on art are not those of the author in 1883, but those of the artist in 1870 to 1875. Harding, a novelist-journalist who appears in all Moore's novels before *Esther Waters,* is closer to Moore, the writer. In fact, Harding, as described in *A Modern Lover,* has had his books "vigorously denounced by the press, as being both immoral and cynical." (How Moore must have wished for such vigorous denunciation!) In the warring art world of *A Modern Lover,* Harding allies himself with the moderns; Lewis Seymour, with the academicians. Moore's sympathies are with Harding: his treatment of Seymour often approaches satire. Yet, curiously, the techniques derived from Moore's art background for use in *A Modern Lover* (i.e., classical balance of elements, methods of characterization, use of color in description) are related to Seymour's, not Harding's, artistic vision.

Despite the fact that in the years 1881 to 1883 Moore openly acknowledged his debt to Zola, there is little imitation of the master of Medan in *A Modern Lover.* Occasional parallels between animal and human nature are drawn; an occasional descriptive passage, such as that of Seymour's Orchard Cottage, is presented with the objectivity of the observer's notebook. But for the most part, as Collet points out, Moore's first novel *"n'offre, en depit, peut-être des intentions de l'auteur, qu'un pâle reflet des théories naturalistes."* Furthermore, on almost every page of *A Modern Lover,* Moore violates an important precept of Zola. *"La naturalisme n'était pas une fantaisie personnelle,"* Zola declared. *"Le romancier expérimentateur . . . ne fait intervenir son sentiment personnel. . . ."* *A Modern Lover* is a highly personal, partly autobiographical book. Its best parts, in fact, as Collet has also observed, are just those pages *"qui relatent les expériences personelles de l'auteur, légèrement transposées."*

Naturalism is present in *A Modern Lover,* however, in the controversy over art. On one side are the academicians, classical artists who had dominated the Royal Academy for centuries. Not in agreement with them, but allied in the struggle against the new moderns, are the medievalists. As the Pre-Raphaelites, they had been the "moderns" of another day. Opposed to both the academicians and the medievalists is a large group which includes musicians and writers. Their common belief is that "the arts are the issue of the manners and customs of the day, and change with those manners according to a general law." Among these, the new moderns, the painters, are the most successful and the most active. Their leader, Thompson, is a naturalist. Explaining his position to a group of painters, among them Lewis Seymour, Thompson declares:

> Ancient art was not, and modern art is, based upon logic. Our age is a logical one, and our art will not be able to hold aloof any longer from the general movement. Already the revolution is visible everywhere. It accomplishes nothing in music that it does not do in painting. The novelist is gaining the day for the study of the surroundings; the painter for atmospheric effects; and the musician will carry the day for melodious uninterrupted deductions, for free harmony, which is the atmosphere of music.

It is Thompson whom Lewis visits, with a letter of introduction from a former teacher, when he first arrives in London. He enters Thompson's studio, expecting to see "graceful nymphs languishing on green banks, either nude or in classical draperies"; instead, he is "regaled with views of housemaids, in print dresses, leaning out of windows, or bar girls serving drinks to beery looking clerks." The walls of Thompson's studio are covered, "not with the softness of ancient, but with the crudities of modern life." It is one of these crudities that Thompson chooses to hang in the Academy in 1879: a large canvas showing a dirty maid-of-all-work in a dirty print dress, pausing in her task of cleaning a dirty doorstep to gossip with the milkmen. "It is the posivitism of art," Frazer, one of Thompson's group, declares admiringly. "At last we have got an art in concord with the philosophy of our age." The open exhibit, everyone knows, is a contest between the moderns and the medievalists. To the moderns, the art of the medievalists is "ideal and subjective."

In an unpublished doctoral dissertation (University of Texas, 1955) Robert J. Barnes has suggested that the moderns of *A Modern Lover* are the painters, writers, and musicians who formed the circle at the Nouvelle Athènes to which Moore belonged when he was in Paris. To the extent that both groups were new, struggling, and opposed to the tradition, they are clearly similar. Correspondences may be noted, in fact, between individual members of the two groups. Frazer, for example, may be linked with Monet, who was principally concerned with atmospheric effects and who painted such works as *Le Gare St. Lazare à Paris;* Thompson's theories are similar to those attributed to Degas in *Impressions and Opinions;* either Renoir,

Manet, or Berthe Morisot might have painted the pic-
nic party in bright colors attributed to Crossley. (Like
Manet, Crossley also painted racehorses.) Collet, however, notes that Moore specifically denied the connection between the moderns and the French impressionists in an article written for the *Hawk* in December,
1889. The ideas expressed by the moderns, Moore said,
were "in the air of London" at the time: no parallel
aesthetic society existed in England.

The artists who expressed the ideas that were "in
the air of London" in the eighteen-seventies, especially
the last half of that decade, were Moore's friends and
acquaintances. Some he had met through his father;
some he had known as an art student in South Kensington and later, at Barthe's classes; some had been, for
brief periods, part of the English colony in Paris and
Dieppe in which there was always a feeling of cama-
raderie. Through them and through his brother Augustus, Moore kept in touch with contemporary British
opinion. While official acclaim was reserved for Academy artists, many who had been rejected by the Academy because of their unorthodox opinions were gaining
support. These were the painters who formed the nu-
cleus of the Grosvenor Gallery exhibitions a few years
later. They were little known in France, according to
Moore's friend, Jacques-Émile Blanche, and they had
little recognition in England, until the World Exhibition of 1878. The pivotal exhibition in *A Modern
Lover* is dated 1879.

Perhaps it was because Moore was supporting one
theory of art and practicing another, perhaps it was be-

cause he was a novice who had not yet thought through the art of the novel but had used what was at hand—*A Modern Lover* is not a unified achievement. Inconsistencies abound in details and events in the three volumes. More serious because more open to the charge of lack of artistry, there are inconsistencies, too, in characterization and in mood. For example, Lewis Seymour of volume three is far more debonair, more consciously manipulative, more purposefully the rake than the Lewis Seymour of the first two volumes. The novel is replete with abrupt shifts of tone, unrelated to incident, throughout. Classical balance may be an attempt to impose unity, but it is an artificial device, unrelated to content. In fact the novel is loosely held together not by devices but by the narrative—as E. M. Forster describes it, the elementary "and then." Moore himself was not insensitive to the deficiencies of *A Modern Lover,* although he often exaggerated the force of the narrative. He realized that although he had declared himself a follower of Zola in public statements and published articles, he had not accorded the master of Medan that sincerest form of artistic approval—imitation.

But Moore's assessment of *A Modern Lover* was the product of hindsight. No doubt at the time of publication the fact that Tinsley had been the publisher of Mary Elizabeth Braddon had seemed a good omen. Miss Braddon's success, however, was not Moore's: public reception of *A Modern Lover* was disappointing as were orders from the circulating libraries, which did not approve of the novel. In 1883 few readers could afford personal copies of novels then published, by convention, in an expensive three-volume format that sold for thirty-one shillings and sixpence. To achieve financial success and wide readership, authors had to respect the straitlaced, moralistic standards of the circulating libraries.

As a means of circumventing library censorship, Zola suggested replacing the conventional format with a cheaper, one-volume edition. Following Zola's suggestion, Moore proposed to Vizetelly, a publisher of foreign books in translation, that he plan a series of one-volume novels that would include Moore's own work. The experiment appealed to Vizetelly, but he was unwilling to assume the entire financial risk. A fortunate fire in the Tinsley warehouse solved the problem. Copies of *A Modern Lover* burned better than they sold, and the insurance money was applied to the cost of publishing *A Mummer's Wife.*

A Mummer's Wife appeared under the Vizetelly imprint late in 1884. (The title page is dated 1885.) Its warm reception encouraged Moore to write *Literature at Nurse,* his famous attack on the circulating libraries. Probably it was Vizetelly's financial success as much as Moore's satiric prose that destroyed the absolute power of the circulating libraries. In any case, *A Mummer's Wife* was a better book than *A Modern Lover,* more deserving of the acclaim it received.

4

A Mummer's Wife:
Zola's Imperfect Ricochet

To gather material for *A Modern Lover,* Moore had plunged deep into his memory, seeking information and anecdotes concerning his own actions and reactions, recalling incidents that revealed the feelings and behavior of Lewis Weldon Hawkins, Jim Browne, and others he had known in the years from 1870 to 1880. His approach to *A Mummer's Wife* was more objective. Years before, Lopez had suggested that he choose for his writings subjects that would astonish the British public. At the time, Moore had considered *Flowers of Passion* an appropriate response, but it was too easily ignored by potential readers. Having read Zola's articles in *Le Voltaire,* however, new possibilities occurred to him. In Victorian England, what kind of life would be most shocking? What part of England would be ugliest, most dismal? What sins most reprehensible? A company of touring actors, he learned, was scheduled to perform *Les Cloches de Corneville* in Hanley and other factory towns. Moore set out with them, an objective observer, eager to see, hear, smell, feel, experience— to be the kind of novelist-journalist that he had portrayed as Harding in *A Modern Lover*. He proposed to write the kind of book that Harding and Thompson had talked about: a contemporary history, an exact and complete reproduction of the social surroundings of a specific time and a specific place, an example of the positivism of art.

The theme of *A Mummer's Wife* was not unfamiliar to English readers of 1885. *Madame Bovary* had crossed the Channel; her English counterpart had emerged in such imitations as *A Doctor's Wife* by Mary Elizabeth Braddon. These were the predecessors of Moore's central character.

As the novel opens, Kate Ede, a dressmaker, is nursing her husband, Ralph, a linen draper, through a particularly virulent asthma attack. In his suffering, Ralph touches Kate far more than he ever has in health. Theirs was not a love match, but an arranged marriage, decided upon by their mothers, two practical, pious women. In her role of angel of mercy, Kate finds the romance that is lacking in their relationship.

In addition to husband and wife, the Ede household consists of Ralph's mother, Mrs. Ede. Miss Henler, Kate's assistant, is there by day; two little girls also come in regularly for sewing lessons. Their dull, routine existence is interrupted by the arrival of a boarder, Dick Lennox, a principal of a touring theater company in town for the week. Mrs. Ede is scandalized that an actor has been welcomed under their roof; Ralph is practical—they need the money; Kate is curious. Secretly, Kate hopes that Dick Lennox will turn out to be the leading man whose picture she has seen on a poster.

Dick Lennox is not the idol that Kate has imagined, but he has sufficient charm to fan the romantic spark already revealed as part of her nature. As a child, while her widowed mother worked in the potteries, she had been cared for by a landlady who delighted in tales of love, sin, and adventure. All her mother's preaching and praying could not counteract such influence. Later, Kate read, not her mother's Bible, but fiction and poetry that fed the tendency toward romanticism which the landlady had nurtured. Kate herself is unaware of the tendency and its dangers: all she knows of life is Hanley; she does not aspire to anything beyond it. In Hanley, in fact, as the wife of a shopkeeper, she is envied by less fortunate young women.

Dick Lennox attempts to seduce Kate. He is an easy-mannered, good-natured man, a bit overweight for a Don Juan, quite clumsy in approach, but charming and debonair to the naïve Kate. She resists—and then, in the days following Lennox's departure, increasingly regrets that she has resisted. However, he has indicated that he will probably return. Kate remembers the stories she used to read about ladies and lovers; she begins to fancy herself as heroine, Lennox as hero. He returns, a series of incidents conspire to encourage their flirtation, and at the end of a week Kate decides to run off with the mummer. She leaves in a romantic fever;

he is phlegmatic—it is time, he thinks to himself, to settle down with a pretty girl, and Kate is as pretty as any he has known.

At first Kate is a stranger among the actors and actresses of the company. But she has a good voice, and before long Lennox finds first bit parts, then larger roles for her. At the beginning, the coarseness of the dressing room distresses her, but with the help of gin, she grows accustomed to it. As her career progresses, Kate becomes more independent, more demanding, more domineering. When her spirit wavers, she turns to gin. It gives her courage, but it also brings out her hysterical-romantic nature. Drunk, she thinks of herself as seduced and abandoned, and she abuses Lennox in her jealous rage. Pregnancy and poverty (the company fails) increase their difficulties, but Lennox remains patient and loyal. After their sickly infant dies, however, and Kate's behavior becomes more violent and erratic, he leaves her with money for support and a promise of reconciliation if she can rehabilitate herself. She fails and soon dies, a coarse, unlovely skeleton of her former self.

One of Zola's techniques which Moore admired especially was his fugal treatment of successive scenes. The inscription of *A Mummer's Wife,* a passage from *L'Introduction Générale à l'Histoire de France* by Victor Durey, suggests that Moore might have considered fugal structure, too: "Change the surroundings in which man lives," whote Durey, "and, in two or three generations, you will have changed his physical constitution, his habits of life, and a goodly number of his ideas." There is, however, as much stasis of personality in *A Mum-mer's Wife* as there is kinesis of environment. Kate does not alter; she is merely stripped down, little by little, to her essential romanticism. She is a simple girl, with neither resources nor defenses. Of people like her, Moore says, "The rich man changes, the peasant remains the same."

A Mummer's Wife is developed pictorially, through a series of related scenes. Each scene of the novel takes Kate Ede for its primary subject. Each shows her struggling with one of the deadly sins. It is an unequal battle, however, because Kate has no moral armor. Again and again, she is betrayed by her own romantic nature. The imagination that helps her nurse her ailing husband selflessly, enjoying her sacrifice, at the start of the book is the same as that which builds in the mirror of her mind the painful image of bereft mother and abandoned woman at the end. Kate may be a victim of her environment, but in large part it is an environment of her own making. Lacking moral strength, she succumbs to every temptation. Her troubles spring chiefly from within. When she finally suffers through her last disfiguring illness and dies, she has experienced disease and death of the spirit as well as of the body. As Moore often tried to point out, *A Mummer's Wife* is really a very moral tale.

In treatment and subject, the scenes of the novel resemble those nineteenth-century engravings which, with various titles relating to sin and virtue, were popular throughout the Victorian era, even into the early twentieth century. Such pictures were the only wall

decorations in the Ede household. This was the era in
which art, for many Englishmen, consisted in Burne-
Jones engravings and graphic representations entitled
Hope, Youth, Love and Death, Life's Illusion, and *Sic
Transit* by George Frederick Watts. Classicism and
medievalism were no longer at war; it was an era, too,
in which a Greek vase could be considered a form of
perfection.

The Greek vase was chosen by George Moore to
represent his conception of perfection in form, and he
applied it whenever he wanted to bestow praise. The
short stories of Turgenev, for example, were to him "as
shapely" as a Greek vase. It was against this image that
he tested his own works. It is not surprising, therefore,
to find in *A Mummer's Wife* the symmetry of a vase.
For Kate Ede, the narrow base of a meager Hanley
existence broadens into a fullness that includes marriage
to a sophisticated man, the admiration of crowds, and
money, then narrows again to Hanley-like surroundings, wretchedness, poverty, and death. All is propor-
tionate: ten chapters are devoted to each of the three
phases to make a total of thirty chapters. Although still
mechanical rather than organic, the structure of *A
Mummer's Wife,* in contrast to that of *A Modern Lover,*
is made to serve theme; the theme is not wrenched to
fit it.

Unfortunately not sustained throughout the novel,
an interesting device that also contributes to the unity
of *A Mummer's Wife* is the symbolic sounding of bells
to herald an important scene or to mark a shift in
narration from present to past. In terms of the story, of

course, the word *Cloches* simply refers to *Les Cloches de Corneville,* the operetta by Planquette which frequently is played by Lennox's company. The circumstances in which the references occur, however, indicate that they function symbolically as well. For example, Kate's assistant mentions *Cloches* just before Lennox arrives. The following day she announces, "Tomorrow they play the *Cloches"*—and the word rings in memories of Kate's childhood and stirs her romantic imagination. *Cloches* is sounded again, in conversation, just before Lennox invites Kate to the theater. Within the limited canvas of Kate's experience, each reference evokes a response, for her imagination is to her mind the "one bit of colour in all those grey tints." On the larger canvas, it is a rudimentary organizing principle; Moore was acquainted with the impressionists' use of tone colors to create musical effects in composition.

References to *Les Cloches de Corneville* in the early sections of the book represent a refinement of attempts at foreshadowing, a device clumsily handled by Moore in *A Modern Lover.* For example, to indicate that Lady Helen will reappear in an important role in a later volume, an "ominous something" descends upon the characters of *A Modern Lover* when her name is mentioned in volume one. The effect is that of an elaborate, disruptive stage whisper. By contrast, as the bells toll at intervals in *A Mummer's Wife,* they fit smoothly into the narrative, yielding the secret of their symbolic significance slowly, through repetition. Not until the middle of the book is it apparent that the bells, indeed, toll for Kate: she scores her first public success in *Les*

Cloches de Corneville; it is also the turning point that marks the beginning of her deterioration. The bells toll again halfway through the last third of the book: drunk and dirty, outside a public house where she has been refused service, she flaunts her filthy petticoats in a grim parody of her first stage success as the simple, naïve, merry Serpolette. The technique is one used more effectively by Moore in the novels after 1905.

Descriptive passages in *A Mummer's Wife* range from a brutal, sharp realism to a vague, romantic impressionism. In the opening lines of the novel, the scene is drawn in minute detail, with strong emphasis on line. There is no color; objects stand out starkly, their outlines clean and well defined. No shade, no tone, mars the effect; it is pure drawing. Later, in the flat light of day, unrelieved by tree or awning or overhanging roof, the town of Hanley is also harsh, forbidding: "No spray of green relieved the implacable perception, no aesthetic intention broke the frigidity of the remorseless angles." Its ugliness is offensive: "The eye was wounded by naked red angles, by the raw green of the blinds, and the similarity of each proportion." In broad daylight, from Wever Hill, the nearby towns are no more appealing. The roofs of Northwood form "a river of black brick unrelieved by any trace of colour saving the yellow chimney-tops that were speckled upon a line of fluffy clouds." Even the windows are black. "So black was everything that even the spire of the church remained a silhouette in the liquid sunlight." At night, however, the ugliness disappears in half light: "the brutal abruptness of the brickwork of the distant

factories was a little blended, just as too hard a drawing is modulated by the passing of a neutral tint over
it; and the deep harmonic measures of monochrome
were broken nowhere, except by the black spires of
Northwood church, which pierced the one band of
purple that yet remained." For those who still look up,
in these dismal surroundings, there is the curve of the
sky and the distant, rolling hills, promising that beauty
has preceded and will outlast the sharp-roofed towns.

The technique of describing the same scene in different kinds of natural light was a favorite with the
impressionists, especially Monet, whose studies of the
cliffs of Etrechat, the Houses of Parliament in London,
haystacks, and Chartres are well known. Carefully taking note of color and light effects, Moore similarly
paints word pictures of the view from Wever Hill. By
day, the lines are sharp, angular; by night, especially
in early evening, they are soft, rounded. Such contrast
between ugliness and beauty was distinguished by
aestheticians and artists of the eighteenth and nineteenth centuries. In England, there had been Hogarth's
Analysis of Beauty, a tract devoted to the superiority
of the serpentine line; in France, Delacroix had pro-
tested the "barbarous invasion of the straight line."

Everything about Hanley is implacably angular and
therefore ugly. Only the soft curve of the distant hills
and the dimmed perceptions of evening reveal to Kate
that there is beauty in the world. The promise is fulfilled as soon as she leaves Hanley: within an hour the
angles begin to disappear, and from the train window
she sees "long soft meadows" reposing "peacefully in

the sunlight." Kate herself undergoes a change during her few happy days with Lennox in Blackpool: "Her figure which had threatened to turn angular, now commenced to swell like a budding flower into delicate roundness." Later, when she is dissipated and dying, Kate reverts to an ugly angularity.

Character delineation in *A Mummer's Wife* is accomplished not only by changes in line, but by references to classical, Italian, and impressionist art. Most are effective, but one description of Kate—as having a complexion "filled with the delicate green of an ostrich egg, and modelled as delicately"—unsuccessfully employs a technique introduced by the Barbizon painters and adopted by the impressionists: that of indicating shadows in complementary colors. The painter, of course, depends on the immediate visual impact of his technique rather than the acceptance of the considered idea: he trusts the eye, not the mind, to admire his green-skinned beauty. The writer presents not the visual impression itself but the technique that creates it: he cannot trust the mind to admire the idea of green-skinned beauty. By emphasizing the color perceived in the shadows, a complement to Kate's flesh tones, rather than the vibrant, sculpted beauty that they indicate, Moore destroys the visual impression he seeks to create and renders the technique ineffective. He cannot count on his readers to "see" Kate as he, with his painter's eye, has seen her.

Moore's ability to construct a character, as he recognized himself, according to Joseph Hone, was always related to his ability to see the character graphically.

Ralph Ede fails to emerge successfully in *A Mummer's Wife;* his portrait is not drawn clearly. Kate, by contrast, is well drawn, despite criticism of the lines mentioned above. Her physical appearance, even in its stages of disintegration, is depicted in detail throughout the novel. Her feelings and attitudes are minutely described, too. All seems consistent. The description of Ralph, however, is often contradictory: he is demanding, selfish, and cold at some times; weak, generous, affectionate at others. Waiting for the train to take them out of Hanley, Lennox and his friends jeer when his name is mentioned. To them, he is a ridiculous figure, small, thin, scrawny. Yet, earlier in the book Ralph is compared by the author to a painting by Michelangelo!

Part of the difficulty is the fact that the narrative method shifts awkwardly from character to omniscient author and back again in the sections dealing with Ralph. Kate's opinions of her husband are presented as those of the author; he expresses Kate's views. Lacking consistency, points of view overlap to produce not complexity, but confusion. The picture is blurred; consequently, the actions and reactions do not always seem appropriate. Ralph's meek acceptance of his wife's departure, for example, and his complete lack of rancor when he meets her years later are not consistent with the domineering, selfish, sarcastic character introduced at the opening of the novel.

Similarly, Dick Lennox is at first characterized as a rake and a trifler; he cheats when the opportunity presents itself; he seems concerned only with his own appetites. Eloping with Kate on the train, and later in Blackpool, he does not give the impression of a man who is deeply in love or consumed with passion. Yet, faced with unemployment, poverty, and an alcoholic wife, he becomes loyal, patient, understanding, industrious, and responsible. The shift in behavior is gradual and steady, however; it is accompanied by frequent references to shifts in environment and physical appearance. Lennox is transformed visibly and therefore more credibly.

Unlike the minor characters in *A Modern Lover*, those in *A Mummer's Wife* receive little attention from Moore. His method in his second novel is the artistic application of light and shadow to focus attention on the subject of a composition and on those aspects of the background which serve to enhance the whole. Background characters, consequently, are left half seen, half drawn.

A Mummer's Wife, in summary, is an artistic improvement over *A Modern Lover* principally because narrative techniques are better related to content. Moreover, the weak and uncertain characterization of Ralph is more than balanced by the memorable characterization of Kate, and the pedestrian prose style (Moore himself later criticized the inaccurate diction, ungrammatical sentences, and unrhythmic prose of his early works) gains strength and vigor from Moore's handling of detail. For these reasons, perhaps, the book was generally well received. Artists and writers who knew Moore chiefly as an artist *manqué* were astonished by the quality of the work. William Ernest Henley praised its realism; Arnold Bennet acknowledged later that it had inspired his own novels about the Five Towns. According to Geraint Goodwin, W. B. Yeats paid Moore the compliment of forbidding his sisters to read the book. Even Susan Mitchell, who was not always an admirer of Moore, conceded that "the fat actor who lures away the poor little woman . . . lives in my memory as one of the most real human beings in English fiction."

As for the British public, it was ready for *A Mummer's Wife*. The Compulsory Education Act of 1870 had brought forth a generation of Kate Edes, who read just well enough to be dissatisfied with their lives; naturalism was in the air; Ibsen was hailed by a growing number of intellectuals; the Fabian Society was promoting socialism among the middle class. Encouraged by the reception of his second novel and interested in social comment through literature, Moore turned to his third novel, already in work, with renewed enthusiasm.

In a letter to Colonel Dease, the State Steward, Moore announced that "the social and political power of the Castle in Modern Ireland" would be the subject of his next naturalistic novel. Deploring the fact that he had not received an invitation to the State Dinner party, he asked that his name be added so that his account might be "as complete, as true, as vivid as possible." At first the request was ignored; Moore persisted; he was refused politely. Moore published his correspondence with the Castle in the anti-Castle *Freeman's Journal* with a commentary that emphasized his intention of working in the manner of *Le Roman ex-périmental*. The publicity given the correspondence on both sides of the Irish Channel established Moore as the "leader of the realistic school in England."

In 1885, however, *Marius the Epicurean* was published in England, and the philosophy of Schopenhauer was attracting English intellectuals. Moore, who often openly confessed his tendency to hunt "many a trail . . . with the pertinacity of instinct rather than the fervour of a reasoned conviction," was partially drawn from the purpose he had stated. The effect of Schopenhauerism was not to reinforce the formula of *le naturalisme, la verité, la science* adopted from the writings of Zola, but to temper Moore's interest in observing the effects of heredity and environment with fascination for the conflicting forces and mysterious depths of the human mind. In 1886, therefore, *A Drama in Muslin* emerged not as a casebook in pessimistic determinism but as an argument for a man to seek alternatives to the ugliness and passion which afflict so much of human existence.

That Moore would be receptive to a philosophy in which will directs life rather than the reverse is evident in the modified Zolaism recorded as far back as *A Modern Lover*. In that novel, Harding scrutinizes Lewis Seymour's room, not so much to see how Seymour was affected by his environment, but to discern in the environment the personal stamp that Seymour had placed upon it. Even in *A Mummer's Wife,* there is a question of how much Kate Ede was destroyed by fate and cir-circumstances and how much she created the fate and circumstances that destroyed her. In *A Drama in Mus-*

lin, character is shown as one of the strong, shaping forces of environment.

On the surface, the novel is about young girls and how their lives are shaped by a convention that makes them, in the opinion of themselves and others, commodities on the marriage market, hunting animals in a chase. (Both metaphors are applied by Moore, directly and indirectly, throughout the book.) The first chapter opens with the graduation exercises of five Galway girls. A phase of their lives has ended. Immediately, preparations are begun for the next, the auctioning-off or husband-hunting phase. It is open season wherever and whenever a young man of sufficient pedigree or income is present, but for the big game, as every parent recognizes, it is necessary to take part in the Dublin season. There, the buyer whom everyone wants to attract, the trophy that everyone wants to capture, is Lord Kilcarney. Mrs. Barton is determined to have him for her daughter Olive. A major portion of the book is devoted to a description of her jungle-market tactics. She is not without obstacles: Olive is almost carried off by a handsome captain of insufficient means; her enemies try to outmaneuver her; and, finally, even though she brings in her heaviest artillery (a sizable dowry), she is forced to concede to Mrs. Scully and her daughter, Violet, who at first seemed no competition at all.

This is the main outline of the "and then" story, but the author, with more skill than he has shown before, weaves the novel of more than one thread. *A Drama in Muslin* is also the story of Lady Cecilia Cullen, who is warped in both mind and body. Her physical deformity precludes her entrance on the marriage market; she develops instead a hatred of men, a cold, perverted passion for Alice Barton, and a religious fanaticism. It is also the story of May Gould, who cannot resist men and therefore cannot hunt by the rules; seduced by Frank Scully, she is helped through her pregnancy by Alice Barton, but character prevails—soon she confesses to having succumbed again, not to love, but to her own overwhelming desire. Alice Barton, the remaining graduate, the most sensitive and intelligent of the five, is the best drawn. Although Moore frequently enters the novel as omniscient author, much of the commentary is presented through Alice, his surrogate. Less attractive than her sister, she is considered inferior goods by Mrs. Barton, who makes little attempt to sell her. She is therefore able to play the role of close observer—subjective to the extent that, like it or not, she *is* on the market; objective to the extent that she does not share her mother's and sister's market values; dependent to the extent that she is a woman; independent to the extent that she finds a way to earn her own income. The irony of the novel is that, having discarded her mother's system of values—which makes marriage the goal of every girl—Alice marries and her sister does not.

The focus of the novel is not so much on events as on character. Whether or not Alice, Olive, Cecilia, Violet, and May find husbands is less important than how they appear against the changing circumstances of their lives. Like a Monet landscape, the five flowers of Galway (the figure is Moore's) are studied in different atmospheric conditions, under changing light.

If the young ladies of St. Leonard's are flowers in an Irish social and political landscape, they are lovely buds at the graduate exercises, half-blown flowers before the Castle ball, full-blown during the Dublin season, and overblown in the year they spend preparing for their second Dublin season. Alice, "like a tall arum lily," had grown in a convent; her name means truth, which is appropriate, but may also refer to sweet alyssum, an unspectacular but pleasant-smelling flower. Olive is a "human flower—roses—carnations" that "a wicked magician had endowed with power of speech." Violet's name has obvious significance; May is the month of flowers. Cecilia, the only one of the five who is neither named for a flower nor described as one, is a fanatically religious girl who despises men and praises chastity. (The saint by the same name, according to medieval legend, took a vow of chastity and encouraged others to do the same through preaching and example.)

The flower that is least spectacular, the one that attracts the least attention, is Alice—whose favorite poem is Shelley's "The Sensitive Plant." The poem is divided into three parts and a conclusion: the first, of twenty-eight stanzas, describes the garden in spring; the second, of twenty-five stanzas, describes the garden in summer; the last, of twenty-eight stanzas, the garden in fall. The conclusion, a six-stanza commentary on the apparent passing of beauty, is chronologically separate. Part one of *A Drama in Muslin,* in which the girls are budding, contains eight chapters; part two, in which they are in full flower, has five chapters; part three, in which they show signs of fading, has eight chapters. The conclud-

ing chapter, chronologically separate, is a commentary
on the rest.

As in the first two novels, specific references to
painters and painting describe the characters of *A
Drama in Muslin,* but a sophisticated development is
their symbolic as well as pictorial value, their connection with thought, action, and ideals as well as physical
appearance. Thus Olive approaches classical perfection,
but lacks the "maternal beauty of the pagan world" in
her face. She is "less human" than a Titian, "less pre-
cise" than a Raphael—"like a figure set by Phidias in
a dream of eternal youth," or like "Fornarina when
not sitting in immortality." She is surely the most
beautiful of the five, as her reception at Dublin Castle
indicates, but there is and always will be something
lacking, although she is "finished," "statue-like." Hers
is not a true, deep beauty; it is "the pseudo-classicality
of a cameo face." By contrast, shy, uncertain Violet
is beauty in the making. She is like "a statuette in bis-
cuit"; she belongs to a period "preceding the apogee
of art"; she has the delicacy, the "exquisite atavism" of
an Indian carved ivory. Mrs. Barton, although still
beautiful and much admired, is the art of the past—
not classical, just a bit out of date. She wears her hair
puffed over her ears in the style of Empress Eugenie;
with her heart-shaped face and her almond eyes, she
might have sat for a portrait by Romney, although
sometimes she is described as more like a Greuze, a
Lely, or a Watteau. She is a pastel—she lacks the solidity
of sculpture, the permanence of oil. Her conversation,
appropriately, is *omelette soufflé;* she disapproves of

Alice's serious reading; she is a charming figure in the fading, frivolous scene that she considers the world to be. Alice Barton is not at all like her mother: lacking conventional prettiness, she has a tall, thin, Pre-Raphaelite figure and Holbein lips. A sound, sensible girl not influenced by her mother's empty values, she marries a sound, sensible doctor who has "a fat Holbein hand." Together they build a comfortable, conventional, middle-class home in which they hang Burne-Jones engravings and reproductions of well-known academic and historical paintings.

Lord Dungory and Arthur Barton are described not only by the paintings they resemble but by the art they approve. The former is a connoisseur; the latter, an artist. In clothing, manner, and conversation, there is something of the last generation about Lord Dungory; yet he wishes to be *au courant* as well. He is a compromise with time, politics, friendship—and obviously, taste in art. His collection is made of a curious assortment; in conversation, he is without a definite point of view. If he has any taste at all, it is determined by two factors: what was established in the past, and what is expensive now. Hence, at dinner, he boasts of his new edition of Tennyson with Doré prints, but when his boorish companion also admires Doré, he changes the subject to Arundel.

Arthur Barton is Lewis Seymour, grown old and foolish. No one since Michelangelo, he assures Alice, could design at he could in his youth. If his work is not appreciated, it is because "the world nowadays" cares only for execution, not conception. At the Academy he finds nothing worthy of his admiration—just laborers' frocks and "a rattle painted to perfection." His own works might be a catalog of the contents of Jim Browne's studio: the large canvases represent Julius Caesar overthrowing the Druids, the bridal of Trier-main, the rape of the Sabines, Samson and Delilah, and Cain shielding his wife from the wild beasts. Alice may have inherited her artistic ability from her father; she has not, however, inherited his quirks. Art, to Alice, is meaningful, useful. Her father paints for no one but himself; she writes articles and stories for magazines and newspapers (aided, incidentally, by the Harding of *A Modern Lover*) .

Descriptive passages in *A Drama in Muslin* reveal the dichotomy of Moore's artistic vision in 1885 to 1886. On the one hand, they are superbly satirical, in the best manner of such artists as Phil May, L. Raven Hill, and S. H. Sime, whose sketches grew steadily more popular during the next ten years. On the other hand, they are lyrical, symbolic, impressionistic, following the work of such artists as Walter Crane, Charles Ricketts, the illustrators of the *Evergreen,* Charles Condor, and Jacques-Émile Blanche. Typical of the former is Moore's description of the marriage market, the "drama in muslin" performed at dinners and parties for which the novel is named. Olive appears at one party "in white silk, so tightly drawn back that every line of her supple thighs and every plumpness of the superb haunches was [sic] seen." A dance, kitchen lancers, is called, and in their irresistible desire "to exercise their animal force . . . , the well-bred hordes charged, intent on each other's overthrow." Mrs. Barton is a wily huntress on such occasions, as she must be, for "in the great matrimonial hunts women have to hunt in packs. At the death they may fight among themselves, and the slyest will carry off the prey; but to ensure a kill at the commencement of the chase a certain *esprit de corps* is necessary, or in the coverts and hidden turns of fashionable life the quarry will slip away unperceived." The Lord Lieutenant greets the participants in the age-old ritualistic hunt in St. Patrick's Hall, Dublin Castle, under a ceiling fresco that depicts St. Patrick receiving the pagans of another time into the true faith.

While Moore's satire is chiefly pictorial, one scene of the novel that relies on the ear rather than the eye owes an obvious debt to Flaubert—specifically to the fair scene of *Madame Bovary:* as Mr. Barton bargains with the tenants outside the house over the question of property values, Mrs. Barton, in the drawing room, haggles with Captain Hibbert over the value of a daughter and a dowry. The two conversations are alternated to give the effect of simultaneity. Moore also attempted passages designed to evoke mood, which included lines such as "The air was full of languor and sorrow, and the evening had all the mystic charm of a fragile maiden poetised by the ravages of a long malady. . . ." No doubt Moore intended, by the lushness of the prose, to contrast the hothouse atmosphere of the convent with the marketplace which the girls were about to enter. But the obvious imitation of "White Nights" from *Marius the Epicurian,* made ridiculous through exaggeration and through juxtaposition with a bare-bones style, had a different effect. Instead of evoking mood, such lines aroused the indignation of critics, who regarded them as "metaphors as monstrous as orchids and as evil in colour," examples of Moore's "maledroit intrusion of the wrong note." Nevertheless it is apparent that Moore had learned that style in writing is akin to brushwork in painting. The result was not immediately successful: he wrote bad prose after *A Drama in Muslin,* but never again did he write the carelessly bad prose of *A Modern Lover* and *A Mummer's Wife.*

A Drama in Muslin was not conceived by Moore as a wholly independent work. The whole of the subject presented in fact was but half of Moore's projected vision. In a prefatory statement to the novel, he declared: " 'A Drama in Muslin' is a study of the life of a group of girl-friends. The men in the story are only silhouettes—a mere decorative background in fact. I propose to write a similar work dealing with a group of young men, in which the women will be blotted out, or rather constitute in their turn the decorative background. In this way I hope to produce two books that will picture completely the youth of my own time." Years later, Lawrence Durrell, another painterly author, wrote the Alexandria Quartet, using a similar concept. Unfortunately, Moore's achievement did not match his artistic vision. Although better written than its predecessors, *A Drama in Muslin* is still a novel limited in large part by an inartistic prose style and by the inability of the author to bring into being all that he could conceive. The paintings of Lewis Seymour, "surpassingly original," as he saw them in his mind's eye, merely conventional when he tried to put them on canvas, are analogous to *A Drama in Muslin*. Frustrated by his failures, the Lewis Seymour in George Moore had given up painting. But the Alice Barton-Harding in him went on, doggedly, determinedly, struggling to write even when he least felt like it, convinced that eventually the ideal would become the real.

5

Sketches in Technique

Lewis Seymour, torn between what was practiced in the studio where he studied and what he learned from Thompson and the moderns, did not know how to approach art. For a long time he could not understand why academic drawings, with every muscle modeled beautifully, was "no species of art" to Thompson, why Frazer painted sunsets violet, why Cassell painted hair blue. Then, having heard their explanations, he became an ardent disciple of the new faith.

In just such a way, George Moore responded to his discovery of style. For a long time, since his early days in Paris, he had known that "the correction of form is virtue." Gautier had been among the first of his idols, and accordingly he had dedicated himself to the correction of form—in the architectural sense, not realizing that it is more than structure. The formlessness that characterized so much of nineteenth-century fiction had sprung, he thought, from a want of structural values; his answer was to bring his story back, according to the principle of eternal recurrence, to the point from which it had started. Once Moore discovered style, however, form took on new meaning. He began to understand that it involved characterization, theme, and prose rhythm as well. The idea was not hard for him to grasp: in painting, he had faced problems of organizing such diverse elements as composition, color, and line into a unified whole. At the same time, again like Lewis Seymour, he was "an ardent disciple in theory, but only faintly in practice." It was hard to shake off the easy, conventional, narrative approach to the novel; it was hard to develop a new one.

From *A Modern Lover* through *A Drama in Muslin*, Moore had been experimenting, developing one device, discarding another. In the works published between *A Drama in Muslin* and *Esther Waters*, Moore seems to be consolidating, perfecting his technique. The characters of the novels of this period are related to characters developed by Moore in the past. The art criticism reveals an attempt to work through attitudes and opinions related to the development of his aesthetic.

The first book to follow *A Drama in Muslin* was *Terre d'Irlande,* published in France in 1886. Much of it had appeared in serial form in a French magazine, *Le Figaro.* Ironically, while Moore was in Brighton, writing a preface for the French edition, he received a letter from Zola, suggesting an Irish book, "a social novel, truthful, audacious, revolutionary." England, he said, would be "consternated by it." Moore's first Irish book had consternated Ireland far more than England; his second, published in English the following year, under the title *Parnell and His Island,* did the same.

In many respects, *Parnell and His Island* is a fascinating and revealing work. Describing Moore's attempts in it to be both subjective and objective, Brown calls it close to "aesthetic schizophrenia." It is an example of Moore's ambivalence, to be sure: as an Irish landlord who, like the Bartons and Kilcarneys of *A Drama in Muslin,* faces ruin as the result of Land League agitation, he condemns Irish peasants and tenant politicians. As the son of George Henry Moore, who gave up his rents during the famine, used his own money for tenant relief, and defended the Fenians in Parliament, he sympathizes with the tenants' problems. As the writer of *Pagan Poems,* he deplores the power of the peasantry to upset gentlemen. As the creator of Alice Barton, as the future author of *Esther Waters,* he is moved by conditions that have caused unrest. *Parnell and His Island* contains whole pages lyrically praising Irish lakes and mountains—and whole pages bitterly denouncing Celt and Catholic.

Moore had gathered material for *Parnell and His Island* during his periodic visits to Dublin and Mayo. After the publication of *A Drama in Muslin,* however, Ireland was no longer hospitable. Many of his Galway friends and relatives accused him of having slandered Irish middle-class life; the possibility that some might be identified with characters or incidents in the book created ill feelings. Moore finished his Irish sketches and composed most of his next novel, *A Mere Accident,* in Sussex, near his friends, the Colville Bridgers.

The hero of *A Mere Accident,* John Norton, is a

strange, dissociated young man, a male version of Lady Cecilia Cullen of *A Drama in Muslin* in some respects. His tastes reveal his personality: Norton buys modern paintings, prefers the music of Wagner and Palestrina, studies the writings of Schopenhauer and the Christian ascetics, and reads Pater. He vows that he will never marry, but his mother insists that he provide the estate with an heir. A mere accident, however, saves him from the bourgeois fate of husband and father: his fiancée, who has been raped by a tramp on the moor, commits suicide.

A brief book limited in vision, far from the tapestry of *A Drama in Muslin,* the story of John Norton was published just four years too soon to be a bona fide product of the "Yellow Nineties," a period in literature and painting characterized by Schopenhauerism, decadence, *fin de siècle* flippancy, and a passion for the outrageous in art and life. The dominant color of the book, recurrent in descriptions and figures of speech, is yellow. Trapped in a mauve and yellow world, yearning for the white radiance of eternity, Norton is clearly a product of the times. "There is a better and a purer life to lead, . . ." he says, "an inner life, coloured and permeated with feelings and tones. . . . I have always been strongly attracted to the colour white."

Spring Days and *Mike Fletcher,* the novels that followed *A Mere Accident* in 1888 and 1889, also focus on character rather than on event. In these books, as Moore had promised in his prefatory note to *A Drama in Muslin,* he concentrates on men: the women are but figures in the background. The central character of

Spring Days is Frank Escott, an artist *manqué* with points of resemblance to both Lewis Seymour and Arthur Barton (therefore, also to George Moore). Escott is a dilettante: he has studied art in Paris, under Bouguereau; he has tried writing poetry and novels; he is an amateur musician. His achievement is limited, however, because essentially he is a connoisseur rather than a true artist. Like Seymour and Barton, he easily finds excuses for his failure: the light, the model, the mood is not right; his art is not sufficiently appreciated; and so on. However, since he can speak with authority about art, he is regarded with respect by Mr. Brooke, whom Moore describes as "a comic King Lear." Like Lord Dungory of *A Drama in Muslin,* Brooke is a collector, but he has even less taste or cultural background. Among his purchases are paintings by Bouguereau, Frith (whose work was represented in the Royal Academy and in Alice Barton's Dublin home), and Linnell, a minor water-colorist. The peripatetic Harding is also a figure in the novel: as surrogate of Moore, he comments cynically on characters and events. On the whole, *Spring Days* is poorly developed and poorly written, but it contains a few memorable passages of description that attempt to render impressions of the same scene at different times of day in prose suited to mood and character.

Mike Fletcher was planned as a sequel to *Spring Days.* Actually a reunion of Moore characters (Escott, Norton, Thompson, Harding, Lady Helen, and Lewis Seymour), it tells the story of the disintegration of a young man of talent and personal magnetism. His prob-

lem is not Kate Ede's, however; the philosophy of
Schopenhauer, not alcohol, is his *bête noire.* The idea
of suicide, of escape from life through denial of life,
fascinates him, as it fascinated Lewis Seymour in the
early pages of *A Modern Lover.* A Byronic Seymour,
in fact, Fletcher is morbidly interested in the self-in-
flicted death of Lady Helen; in the end, he, too, shoots
himself. Like Seymour, Fletcher is also George Moore.
Born of an Irish mother and a French father, he is
twenty-nine, and he has published a volume of verse
and two comedies. George Moore's cultural "parents"
were Ireland and France; at twenty-nine, he had published two volumes of poetry and one play.

Art is a major subject of conversation among the
characters of *Mike Fletcher.* All together and in various
combinations, Escott, Thompson, Norton, and Fletcher
discuss their different tastes and different points of
view. Norton holds forth on such diverse topics as
Byzantine art, the Italian Renaissance, and the paintings of Corot. Thompson, still a spokesman for the moderns, declares opinions attributed to Degas in *Impressions and Opinions.* Fletcher, essentially a romantic,
analyzes a tapestry for Lady Helen in terms of the real
and the ideal.

As in earlier novels, art is used in *Mike Fletcher* to
establish points of reference for description. London
looks like a Whistler etching; the scene in the music
hall resembles a painting in the Dutch manner; the
characters themselves are compared with Greek statuary,
the sculptuie of Gougon, and paintings by Botticelli,
da Vinci, Raphael, and Watteau. Both discussion of

art and description of character and environment are used in *Mike Fletcher,* however, to support the concept that character dominates environment. Moore goes beyond the mere cataloging of apartment furnishings to reveal taste: London to Mike Fletcher is in accord with Fletcher's mood; London to John Norton corresponds to Norton's mood. Harding explains why: "We find but ourselves in all that we see and feel. The world is but our idea. . . ." Such correspondence between character and environment, in which the mood of the character determines the nature of the perception of the environment, is probably what Moore had in mind when he wrote to his mother a letter quoted by Joseph Hone (*Life of George Moore,* p. 150) : "My novel is a new method. It is not a warming up out of Dickens and Thackeray. It is a method that will certainly be adopted by other writers, but will the first effort meet with recognition. I scarcely think so. . . ."

Vain Fortune, the last novel to appear between *A Drama in Muslin* and *Esther Waters,* has no narrative connection with *Spring Days* and *Mike Fletcher;* apparently Moore dropped his idea of a trilogy. It is interesting primarily for the information that it provides concerning Moore's working habits in the 1890s. No longer was he the author of *A Modern Lover,* eager to put down his story, from beginning to end; no longer was it sufficient to have a good story to tell. Method was his chief concern.

Vain Fortune was originally serialized in the *Lady's Pictorial,* then published in book form in England. When Scribner's announced its intention of issuing an

American edition, Moore begged permission to make changes, for he was dissatisfied with *how* he had told his story. (The story itself remained the same.) Shortly after the new American version appeared, a Dutch publisher expressed interest in the book. Moore recommended the Scribner's *Vain Fortune* as superior to the original English version, but the Dutch translator, pointing to advantages in each, asked Moore to approve a third version that would combine the two. Moore agreed: the 1895 Walter Scott edition was the result.

The publishing history of these early editions of *Vain Fortune* is an important chapter in the history of Moore's growth as a serious writer. By 1895 he had progressed from his role as mere teller of tales to that of craftsman. Parallel to his development was the growth of his understanding and appreciation of art trends and techniques. Letters and essays of the period and conversations recorded in retrospect reveal his interest in the analogy of the arts: the "spiritual perversity" of Verlaine's poetry, which sprang "lilylike" from his sick mind; the qualities of Holbein and Hogarth in Balzac's *Une Vielle Fille;* the landscapes of Corot and the characters of Gainsborough in Turgenev's short stories; and the Pre-Raphaelite minuteness of detail of Flaubert and Holman Hunt. Chekhov, to Moore, had the delicacy of a water-colorist; Dostoevsky's work was like "sculpture in snow" or "soft clay which is apt to crumble."

The most significant new title published during this period, however, is not one of those mentioned above but the first (1888) edition of *Confessions of a Young Man,* an impressionistic autobiographical novel narrated by Edward Dayne. Digressive and fragmented, with a shifting style, in 1888 it purported to be the memoirs of a young aesthete whose Irish childhood, English education, and Parisian introduction to life owed much to the fictional and real life models previously mentioned—including the fictional and real life George Moore. Noting that in later life it was hard for Moore himself to distinguish fact from fiction in *Confessions of a Young Man*—especially as it grew and developed through revision after revision—John Freeman acknowledged that he would not undertake such a task and suggested that it was indeed beyond any critic or biographer. The problem was the way in which Moore made use of biographical details: the biography of mind and emotions, of wishful thinking and inward desire, served equally with more conventional biographical materials. But what was real? Anticipating twentieth-century experiments in fiction and film, Moore understood that the world of the mind and the emotions is as real as the physical world; wishes, dreams, and daydreams, incidents enjoyed or suffered vicariously, are as much part of man's past as anything perceived through the five senses. Besides, the biographical details were of no factual importance: they were but Forster's table and chairs, out of focus because they were not the artist's subject. The true subject of *Confessions of a Young Man* was the young George Moore: the slim book was an attempt to recreate the atmosphere of his mind. Thus Moore the novelist revised and expanded *Confessions of a Young Man* at least four times before his death, first as early as 1889 when he acknowledged his subject by changing the name of the narrator to George Moore, but never did he change its atmosphere. Dayne-Moore remains through every revision the "disagreeable young man of bad education" described in an *Academy* review of the first edition. Although in later novels and other purportedly autobiographical works Moore freely used —and freely altered—incidents from life as it was lived by himself, Lewis Hawkins, Bernard Lopez, and others, the accounts given in *Confessions of a Young Man* remained essentially the same. Moreover, all additions to the revised editions were in keeping with the original spirit of the work which has been regarded by some critics as an early "portrait of the artist as a young man."

6

Esther Waters:
A Tale That Marks a Period

In an eightieth-birthday letter to George Moore published in the *Times* of London, *Esther Waters* was acclaimed by a group of English artists, writers, and critics as a "tale that marks a period in our literature." It was, after *Confessions of a Young Man,* Moore's next significant publication. A year earlier, in 1893, *The Strike at Arlingford* had been produced and printed. While not the success that Moore had hoped it would be, *The Strike at Arlingford* proved that Moore was by no means a failure as a dramatist: the "play in three acts" was praised by William Archer, and it brought offers for other plays. But Moore's chief concern from 1893 to 1894 was the "story about servants" that had been teasing his imagination ever since the "awful Emma" of *Confessions of a Young Man* met her lover on the way home from the public house "with the beer for missus' dinner." In 1893 preliminary chapters appeared in the *Pall Mall Gazette.*

But the Esther of "Passages from the Life of a Work-girl" was closer to the Beggar Girl of *Pagan Poems,* Emma of *Confessions of a Young Man,* the laundress of Moore's Temple days, Gwynnie of *A Modern Lover,* and May Gould of *A Drama in Muslin* than to the strong, enduring Esther of the novel. As she emerged in 1894, Esther's fictional cousins are Alice Barton of *A Drama in Muslin,* Rose Leicester of *The Lake,* and Heloise of *Heloise and Abelard.* It is this Esther who gives the novel its stamp of individuality. As the story progresses Esther ages: a girl of twenty when the novel opens, she is a woman of nearly forty at its end. But the eternal, unchanging aspect of her nature is emphasized by her name: she is a strong, true river of life. The years of her life flow into the future as the waters of the river flow into the sea. Thus the future becomes the past, yet the river remains, perhaps reflecting a star (Esther) in its surface, symbol of steadfastness and eternity.

Esther Waters, however, is not only the story of Esther's struggle against overwhelming obstacles to bring up her illegitimate son, Jackie, in a hostile society. It is also the story of the Barfield family, ruined by gambling and horse racing, and of the temptations and troubles its members have brought into the lives of others. It includes an account of baby-farming practices and the treatment accorded poor unwed mothers in Victorian England. It contains a vignette of Miss Rice, a spinster writer, whose life is that of the sheltered gentlewoman, but who has come to understand much that she has not experienced through empathetic observation of her servants. And it is a picture of Ireland and England, country and city, parlor and pantry, just before the turn of the century.

Much has been written about the ending of *Esther Waters,* which begins with a repetition of the opening lines: it is not a conclusion but a return. At first glance this technique may seem similar to that used in opening and concluding passages of *A Modern Lover:* Gwynnie appears in the final chapter to retell the events of the first three chapters. But as she is portrayed at the end, Gwynnie is utterly different from the character portrayed at the beginning; there is no suggestion of a recurrence of events; and the characters stand to one another in totally new relationships. Gwynnie is so changed, in fact, that she is not recognized, although she has been a servant in the Seymour household since Lewis's marriage to Lady Helen. Seymour has completely forgotten the promise he once made to her, and neither he nor the reader is reminded of it. In contrast, the opening and closing chapters of *Esther Waters* emphasize the sameness of character and setting. Esther came to Woodview in the bloom of youth; she returns in the autumn of her life. She arrived at the beginning on a warm, sunny day; the grass, the flowers, the trees were all surging with life, and the warm blood in Esther responded. She returns on a bleak, cold day in November, no longer pulsing with the sap of life, but like the evergreens, whipped by the same wind, enduring. Except for the normal alteration of season, neither she nor Woodview has changed; the house itself and its mistress show the effects of the years, but they, too, are essentially the same. Esther has come full circle, but this is not the end of her story. She is content with Mrs. Barfield, and eventually old age will overtake her, but the novel ends, symbolically, not in November but in February. There is talk of fixing up the garden and sowing vegetables as soon as the cold weather breaks. The grass has not yet begun to grow, Esther observes, but already the land has the gray-green look of early spring. Impelled by an instinct as old as the cosmos, the same kind of instinct that has driven Esther through all the hard years of her life, the rooks begin to gather twigs for their nests. And then Jackie, a handsome young man in the uniform of a soldier, comes to visit Esther. She has endured; through Jackie she will continue to endure.

Esther Waters is not, then, a novel of pessimistic determinism. Heredity and environment do not take their expected toll of Esther and her son. She obeys a stronger law. "The hardness of life as she experiences it is mitigated for the reader by a sense of the essential fineness of human nature," writes Joseph Beach. She has a "primordial, almost protoplasmic, strength which would survive all persecutions and outlive her persecutors," explains Malcolm Brown, "an attitude similar to William Faulkner's conception of the Negro servant, Dilsey." The passing years provide the outline of her story; the incidents in Esther's life, *les masses:* Esther herself is the unifying element. The result is the integration of character, structure, and content, the achievement of organic form.

Heredity and environment do control the lives of other characters in the book, however. Behind the

monumental figure of Esther Waters, there stretches a
frieze of minor characters, neither half-drawn, like the
minor characters of *A Mummer's Wife,* nor minutely
described, like those of *A Modern Lover,* but sculptured
in relief against a background that is as much a part
of them as a block of stone is part of the figures that
are carved upon it. The father of Esther's husband,
William Latch, for example, was the steward of the
Barfield estate; he gambled away his earnings, embez-
zled money to pay his gambling debts, and was saved
from prison only by his wife's offer to forego her cook's
wages until the stolen sum was repaid. The gambling
fever is in William's blood. In addition, since his mother
has to stay at Woodview where she has forfeited her
wages, her son has to stay there with her. It is a perni-
cious environment, in which horse racing is almost
everyone's major concern. When the Barfields suffer
heavy losses, after Esther has left, the other servants
are dismissed, too. But they continue the life they
learned at Woodview, gambling and drinking. Old
John, the Barfields' butler, once waited upon by lower
servants, is reduced to begging; in his old age, his sav-
ings gone, there is only the workhouse before him.
Sarah Tucker, in love with a gambling man, turns to
prostitution and eventually steals from a new employer
to supply her lover with betting money. Not even the
members of the Barfield family escape the curse of
heredity and environment. When young Arthur comes
to the King's Head, Esther observes that he has lost not
only his inheritance but also the look of a gentleman.

Yet like his father, he continues, to his mother's dismay, a breeder and racer of horses.

In 1894 many reviewers received *Esther Waters* as *"un ricochet de Zola en Angleterre."* Moore seemed to corroborate their opinions by insisting later that it was an "English story" based on his observations of "the simple sturdy steadfastness of the Saxon race," and a number of critics have documented what appears to be the foundation of its "Englishness": the identification of Woodview, the home of the Barfields, where Esther works as kitchen maid, with Buckingham, the Sussex home of Moore's friends, the Bridgers; the identification of Mrs. Barfield with Mrs. Bridger; the picture of Esther's life in London after she leaves Woodview; descriptions of characters, scenes, and conversations drawn, according to Moore's biographers, from London betting parlors; and the identification of Esther herself with Emma, "the horrible servant" of Moore's *Confessions of a Young Man,* or with the loquacious laundress of Moore's Temple days, or with Gilbert Frankau's wet nurse, or, most recently, with Maggie Younghusband, purported to be the author of "From the Maid's Point of View," an article published in the August, 1891, issue of the *New Review.* These arguments, however, are dubious: further examination reveals that Woodview owes as much to Moore Hall as to Buckingham; events and stories from Moore's Mayo days have been woven into the narrative; Irish men and Irish women have sat for portraits, or at least character studies, in the novel; and Esther herself may be a composite of unfortunate

girls, some from Mayo, whom Moore knew personally
or with whose stories he was acquainted. Inevitably, if
such contradictory evidence is accepted, it must lead to
a critical reexamination of *Esther Waters*. For a study
of the effects of heredity and environment, of characters
and situations drawn from notebook observations by an
objective author, makes for one kind of fiction—and recollections of events, people, and places, selected and
recombined by a subjective author from scenes of his
childhood, make for another.

The evidence for Irish elements in *Esther Waters*
begins to present itself in the very first pages of the
novel. From the outside, Woodview, the "Italian house"
is, of course, Buckingham, the home of the Bridgers,
which Moore used also in earlier novels. Moore Hall,
a Georgian mansion, was without urns and gables and
ornamental porches; it would not fit Moore's description. But as soon as Esther walks through the yard outside the kitchen, she passes from Sussex to Mayo, from
Buckingham to Moore Hall. Similarities include the
size and location of the kitchen, the large range, the
shelves reaching to the ceiling, which were "covered
with a multitude of plates and dishes." It was at Moore
Hall, as at Woodview, that horses were brought through
a long, covered passage to be washed down in the courtyard just outside the kitchen. As for the number and
purpose of outbuildings, no doubt the Bridgers kept
sufficient horses for their own personal use, but it was
George Henry Moore, father of the novelist, who ordered the construction of a row of stables to house the
racehorses that he bred. On a grassy hill near the Bar-

field house, William points out for Esther the racecourse where the Gaffer's thoroughbreds are trained and tried. From the long windows of the drawing room at Moore Hall, the racecourse used by George Henry's horses is still barely discernible beyond the trees.

Other aspects of Woodview are related to other memories from George Moore's childhood. In 1861 Croaghpatrick, the "Silver Braid" of the Moore stables, was entered for the Stewards' Cup at Goodwood in Sussex. About a month before the race, George Henry Moore, his wife, and his eldest son followed Croaghpatrick to Hednesford, where the horse had been committed to the care of a trainer. George Moore loved the stables at Cliff's; he was given his own pony to ride across the downs; his companions were stable boys; his days were passed among horses; his evenings were full of talk of them.

Once Woodview is recognized as a multiple vision, a combination of memories, it is easier to see that characters of the novel have been created in similar fashion. As Buckingham is the model for the exterior of Woodview, Mrs. Bridger serves outwardly as a model for Mrs. Barfield; as aspects of Moore Hall form the interior of Woodview, so characteristics of Moore's mother and grandmother govern the words and actions of its mistress. When Esther first meets her employer, she sees "a little red-haired woman, with a pretty, pointed face"; her hair, "growing thin at the parting," is "smoothed back above the ears." Although nearing fifty, she is still as slight as a young girl. Parallel passages in "A Remembrance," a sketch first published in the *New Review*,

later included in *Memoirs of My Dead Life,* describe
Mrs. Bridger: "It was in the vastness of Westminster
Hall that I saw her for the first time—saw her pointed
face, her red hair, her brilliant teeth"; "She was now
fifty-five, but such an age seemed impossible for so girl-
like a figure and such young and effusive laughter";
". . . the sunlight fell on the red hair, now grown a little
thinner. . . ."

But Mrs. Barfield was a deeply religious woman, a
member of the Plymouth Brethren who gathered her
"woman-servants for half-an-hour every Sunday afternoon" to "instruct them in the life of Christ." Mrs.
Bridger, on the contrary, surprised Moore by "her mani-
fest want of interest in the discussion of religious problems." No more satisfaction was he able to get from his
own mother who, according to an anecdote in *Confessions of a Young Man,* apparently would not be baited
by Moore's declarations of atheism and anti-Catholicism.
Stories that Moore had heard about his grandmother,
however, and her letters to his father, suggest that she
was borrowed for the religious aspect of the portrait of
Mrs. Barfield. To be sure, it was Louisa Moore, of all
the women in George Moore's life, who was most opposed to anything related to racing. She had lost one son,
John, in a riding accident; in vain she had tried to keep
her other sons away from horses. But George Henry,
father of the novelist, would not be dissuaded, not even
by the death of a second brother, Augustus. To the end
of her days, which continued into the life of her eldest
grandson, Louisa Moore never ceased protesting against

the racing activities of her son and the breeding of horses at Moore Hall.

Mary Moore's concern was not horse racing but gambling. Her husband, she knew, had almost ruined himself as a young man in England; she was dismayed when her eldest son soon found his way to the betting parlors after the family moved to London. But her influence was weak, for like the Gaffer, George Henry Moore had been a racing man before she had met him; like Ginger, George Augustus Moore had been brought up with horses and horse talk so that both were a part of his natural environment. Mary Moore seems, moreover, to have been less determined, less inclined to control others, than her mother-in-law. Describing the effect of her death in 1895 upon the novelist, Joseph Hone writes that "her Catholic piety was as sweet natured and unintellectual as the evangelicism of Mrs. Barfield." Hers was the patience of "The Saint," the calm understanding, the ability to give sympathy to those with whom she did not agree.

Of the other characters in the book, John Randal is easily identified: the evidence for connecting him with the butler of Moore Hall is so strong as to be without question. Like Mr. Leopold, Joseph Applely, an ex-jockey, had been in the service of his master long before either was married. And like Mr. Leopold, he was a source of advice and anecdotes about gambling and racing for the young master. Maurice Moore has described this curious and colorful man as small and secretive. About him there was always an aura of mystery;

his pronouncements on horses were "never said above a whisper." Mary Moore disliked Applely—as Mrs. Barfield disliked Mr. Leopold. But Applely's relationship with George Moore, before the family removed to London, apparently was as close as that of Mr. Leopold and Ginger. Like Moore, Ginger had "pale yellow hair which gave him a somewhat ludicrous appearance." Unlike Moore, Ginger was allowed to ride in the trials —a bit of wishful thinking, no doubt, on the part of the author whose own boyhood dreams of becoming a jockey had not been realized. The Gaffer, an excellent horseman and the only one able to command Mr. Leopold's respect, is also the only one who trusts Mr. Leopold. The nature of their relationship plus the fact that the Gaffer is master of Woodview and father of Ginger suggests, of course, that he is a fictional counterpart of George Henry Moore.

Much of the talk about horses and horse racing in the early part of the novel is concerned with the winning of the Stewards' Cup at Goodwood—the race that had brought Croaghpatrick, George Henry Moore, Mrs. Moore, and young George to Sussex in 1861. The story of the trials and the race itself, as recounted later by Maurice Moore, closely parallels the story of Silver Braid's triumph as it is described by Mr. Leopold in *Esther Waters*. Maurice Moore also states as fact that "many of the characters in 'Esther Waters' were drawn from the jockeys and racing servants at Moore Hall at this time."

Identification of William Latch as a character out of Moore's Irish past contributes to the evidence of the novel's Irish background. William was drawn from the second man at Moore Hall whom Colonel Moore described as "an excellent servant . . . but with rather primitive manners." He was probably the same man with whom the young George Moore "used to have great disputes about the Stakes"—disputes won by Moore, apparently, according to a letter to Appely quoted by Joseph Hone. In 1873 William accompanied Moore to Paris. The name given on his passport was Moloney. (Moore, for whom spelling was never a strong point, calls him Mullowney in *Confessions of a Young Man* and *Hail and Farewell.*) Dismissed by Moore, he returned not to Mayo but to London. William Latch also goes to Paris, not as a valet, but as the husband of Peggy Barfield, a young relative of the Barfields with whom he elopes. He, too, is dismissed—his wife takes a lover—but he is able to find a good situation for himself in London as part owner of a public house.

Esther is also identified by Moore in his preface to the dramatic version of *Esther Waters,* published in 1913, as "a fellow servant of Latch and Randal." With underservants of the household in which she is employed, on the street observing others like herself, even in the workhouse, Esther maintains a strong sense of dignity, an independent pride, and a system of values that set her apart from the other servants. Throughout the novel there are occasional references to Esther's "race," sometimes specified as *Saxon,* but her features are those of the Celtic stereotype (cf. L. P. Curtis, *Anglo-Saxon and Celt,* New York, 1968), and every description of appearance or character reveals her as different from her fellows. Esther does not read, yet her speech is for the most part more courteous, prettier, more refined than the Cockney she hears around her. Both she and William frequently use the attributive *and* construction characteristic of Anglo-Irish dialect. By contrast, the other servants speak a Cockney dialect indicated by omission and intrusion of *h* sounds and by substituting *ter* for *too* and *yer* for *you*. While Esther, too, lapses into such speech on rare occasions, it is used consistently in the dialogue of others.

As for Esther's religion, which Moore identifies as Plymouth Brethren, it is very like the harsh Catholicism described by him in "Julia Cahill's Curse," a story from *The Untilled Field*. Moreover, after having Esther explain to Sarah Tucker that members of her sect do not use prayer books, he includes a prayer book among her belongings. Moore also has Esther baptize the dying infant whom Mrs. Spires is trying to hasten to an early grave—an error that he discovered by the time the 1899 edition was in preparation. (In this and subsequent editions, Esther tells Mrs. Spires that infant baptism is "not the way with the Lord's people. . . . You must wait until it is a symbol of living faith in the Lord.")

Other lapses in the first edition, some never corrected, strengthen the impression that Moore was working, in *Esther Waters,* not from notebook observations but from memory. What "scientific investigations" were necessary, in fact, he accomplished somewhat haphazardly. For example, Moore seems unaware of the fact that in the London of the late nineteenth century Esther could have gone to a charitable hospital that did not require a letter of recommendation from a subscriber. And it is doubtful that he ever tried to trace on foot the path that Esther takes when, heavy with child, she seeks her letter of recommendation. Even at a brisk trot she could not have followed the route that he describes, setting out after midday dinner from her mother's home near the Vauxhall Bridge Road, stopping frequently to ask directions, waiting to be interviewed in hospital and subscribers' homes, telling her story upon demand, and arriving at the Marble Arch on an April day at sunset. Eliza Aria (*My Sentimental Self,* London, 1922) writes of Moore's Zolaesque method of gathering information for his hospital scenes, but in fact the race at Goodwood and the Derby scenes are recounted in more vivid— and for the most part more accurate—detail. Silver Braid wins by a head in a racing victory almost identical with that of Croaghpatrick, but Esther's labor pains come (most curiously!) first from between the shoulders and then from the knees—and at intervals just before Jackie's birth that bear no resemblance to a normal confinement. Nine days of hospital life pass in one paragraph; then Esther's sister Jenny comes with news of their mother's death. Following Jenny's visit, four more days pass in another brief paragraph, and the gates of the hospital close behind new mother and child.

The inescapable conclusion is that *Esther Waters* is not naturalistic, nor does it depend for its material on the techniques of the realists. There are, to be sure, echoes of Zola and Flaubert, especially in passages dealing with Sarah Tucker and Margaret Gale, and something of Turgenev perhaps in the manner in which

Esther endures. But to the extent to which it is an Irish story, set against a background from Moore's childhood and early youth, developing character from people he used to know, recreating scenes and events with which he was familiar through direct experience or through stories told to him, *Esther Waters* is a modern novel, a work that employs narrative methods and aesthetic principles further developed in *The Untilled Field* and *The Lake.*

Seven years after the novel appeared, Moore moved to Dublin. It may have been hatred of the Boer War that drove him from England; it may have been the desire to join Yeats and Martyn in their new enterprise. But another possibility is that the voices heard by Moore in the Chelsea Road, urging "Go to Ireland! Go to Ireland!" had been whispering to him for some time, even as he was writing his so-called English story, *Esther Waters.*

7

A New Century,
A New Style

George Moore's position in the literary and art worlds
of 1894 to 1905 was a curious one. More than any of his
earlier works, *Esther Waters* established him as a writer
of importance in his own time. The publication of his
novels no longer brought forth cries of surprise from
his contemporaries: his record of achievement was sub-
stantial. Including *Esther Waters*, by 1894 Moore had
signed his name to three published plays (five, if *Worldliness* is counted and the libretto translation of *Les
Cloches de Corneville* is included), two volumes of
poetry, eight novels, one fictional autobiography, one
collection of essays about Ireland, and two collections
of essays about art and literature. All his early fiction
had been issued in numerous editions by different pub-
lishers in both England and the United States; moreover, there were newspaper and magazine articles, pam-
phlets, and prefaces to his credit. In his early years,

Moore's penchant for appearing ridiculous (*ma petite luxe,* he called it) had created talk about him. After 1894, his talent for making enemies helped to keep his name before the public, as those he had offended criticized and denounced him.

The Byronic side of Moore's nature delighted in denunciation: in fact, his friends have reported that he encouraged the circulation of stories about himself. He had at the time a close circle of friends, influential and widely respected members of the Irish, English, and French intellectual communities. Outside this group in which Moore's idiosyncrasies and shifts of opinions were regarded for the most part with humor and tolerance, no one could be certain of his support. No one knew which of his idols he would break next—which artistic cause he would next espouse. The one true devotion he seemed to have was to Manet, Degas, and the impressionists. Together with such men as D. S. MacColl and Hugh Lane, he was among the first to urge the exhibition and sale of their works in England.

Except for superficial examples of impressionist influence, however—descriptive passages in which Moore views a scene in the impressionist manner or as one of the other modern painters would have executed it, dialogue discussions of art in which Moore's sympathies are apparent, brief and tentative attempts to weave outward and inward consciousness into an artistic whole—Moore's approach to style and structure in writing in 1894 seems closer to the graphic art techniques learned at the Salon Julien than to those discussed at the Nouvelles Athènes. To read his novels and his art criticism published between 1883 and 1894 is to suspect him, in the words of Malcolm Brown, of "aesthetic schizophrenia."

At this point, however, Moore again embarked on a period of experimentation similar to that which marked the period preceding the publication of *Esther Waters*. Again he seems to have been intrigued with the idea of the analogy of the arts. Association with Arthur Symons, an apostle of the symbolists and of their attempts to assimilate poetry, music, and painting, perhaps reawakened his interest. Years before, in *A Modern Lover,* Moore had written into Thompson's conversation a comparison of the different effects produced on the aesthetic sense by music, art, and drama. The result of Moore's new concern for analogy in art was a projected work, first conceived as one novel, later published as two: *Evelyn Innes* and *Sister Teresa*. Stylistically, *Celibates,* published in 1895, stands in relation to these novels as *Parnell and His Island* stands in relation to the novels published between 1887 and 1892: it was an exercise in the exploration of ideas and the development of technique. A transitional book, in some respects it is related to Moore's earlier fiction; in others, it anticipates his future work.

The central theme of *Celibates* is the reverse of that presented in *Esther Waters:* the three characters for whom the three independent stories are named suffer from a weak rather than a strong life force. Thus they are prey to diverse emotional impulses, victims of their environment.

"Mildred Lawson," revised from "An Art Student"

(*Today,* spring, 1895), is an attempt to reveal, through outer manifestations, the inner world of an artist *manqué:* like her predecessor, Lewis Seymour (and like Moore himself), Mildred has "a dash of genius." She studies at a studio that resembles the Salon Julien; her art training is objective, academic, semiclassical. Her friends, however, have discovered the Barbizon artists who paint in color rather than in black and gray. Significantly, much of the dialogue between Mildred and her friends concerns method in painting reflections and shadows. Mildred is in conflict: she hesitates to accept the new methods embraced by her friends so enthusiastically; at the same time, she hesitates to accept the life that is offered by her lover. Indecision and reluctance to change characterize her behavior in all aspects of life.

"John Norton," a revised and condensed version of *A Mere Accident,* is unified by character and color. As in the original version, yellow, the fashionable color of the period, recurs frequently in descriptive passages; John's character is still ascetic, perverse; his fascination with death—specifically, with Kitty's death—still dominates the narrative. (It is also reminiscent of the George Moore of *Pagan Poems,* the author of "Ode to a Dead Body.")

Agnes Lahens, the central character of the third story, escapes her parents (who resemble Mr. and Mrs. Barton of *A Drama in Muslin*) by entering a convent. Moore once described Esther Waters as another Alice Barton; Agnes is the reverse of the coin: weak, supersensitive, timid. Her story is presented in chiaroscuro: the purity of Agnes contrasts with the worldliness of her mother, the peace and love of the convent with the tension and bitterness at home.

Moore's achievement in *Celibates* is his development of symbolic themes (i.e., the yellow world of John Norton, the art-life analogy in "Mildred Lawson," etc.). Although *Celibates* was not well received, Moore always regarded it more favorably than did his critics. Its themes and character-types continued to appear in other novels and stories, and in later years he revised it, first as *Celibate Lives*, then as *In Single Strictness*. By contrast, his next two novels, which he regarded as failures in retrospect, never were admitted to authorized editions of his work, despite the fact that the first, at least— *Evelyn Innes*—was an immediate financial success. At the time of publication, however, he wrote of both with characteristic enthusiasm.

Evelyn Innes is the story of another Mike Fletcher. Evelyn lives fully, sensuously, abandoning herself to all aspects of the life force that gushes within her; yet she is dissatisfied. She is intense in love and in music, but neither provides the peace she requires or the fulfillment she craves. Finally, she seeks an end to inner torment, not in self-realization, but in self-denial. Like Agnes Lahens, Cecilia Cullen, and John Norton, Evelyn turns to religion.

Evelyn Innes is George Moore's third nun and his first musical artist. Before her, John Norton had been sincerely interested in music, but his talent was limited—he was another artist *manqué*. Thompson, the minor figure of *A Modern Lover* who speaks on so many major subjects, considered music without literature an art incapable of expressing more than generalities. Between 1883 and 1895, however, Moore had met Edouard Dujardin, founder and co-editor of *La Revue Indépendante* and *La Revue Wagnérienne*. It was Dujardin who introduced Moore not only to the music of Wagner but also to the musical devices that, translated into prose techniques, contributed to the development of Moore's last style.

Dujardin was an aesthete: Jacques-Émile Blanche describes him as wearing a waistcoat of amaranth-colored velvet with gold buttons and a pleated necktie knotted *en jabot.* He was a bookseller, a publisher, an editor, a writer of symbolist plays, an actor (in his own plays), a poet, a novelist, and a biblical scholar. Moore (and Joyce after him, if Joyce's dubious testimony is to be believed) learned from Dujardin's novel, *Les Lauriers sont coupés,* the technique of the interior monologue. It was Dujardin also who provided Moore with the technical details he needed for the writing of *Evelyn Innes, The Brook Kerith,* and *Heloïse and Abelard.* The French translation of Moore's *Confessions of a Young Man* was published in *La Revue Indépendante* before its financial collapse.

Evelyn Innes owes to Dujardin not only the character of a serious musician and the information needed to sustain one, but also its experimental structure. As Moore noticed, Dujardin had developed *Les Lauriers sont coupés* through a progression of thematic statements connected by restatement, variation, and contrast. In *Evelyn Innes* and *Sister Teresa* Moore attempted to imitate Dujardin; his approach was hesitant and he did not achieve outstanding success. Afterwards, however, the musical arrangement of elements learned from the Frenchman became the basis of his later prose style. Combining terms derived from music and painting, he called it "the melodic line."

While Moore was writing *Evelyn Innes,* W. B. Yeats and Edward Martyn were trying to found an Irish theater. As a beginning, each had written a play—Yeats, *Countess Cathleen;* Martyn, *The Heather Field.* Moore had been an admirer of the work of Yeats for several years. Martyn was a distant cousin and an old friend. Yeats and Martyn knew that Moore's literary reputation and dramatic experience would be an asset to their project: together, they suggested his return to Ireland. The author of *Parnell and His Island* was receptive: he had portrayed Ulick Dean, Sir Owen Asher's rival in *Evelyn Innes,* a dreamy-eyed mystic who spoke of Celtic gods and other worlds, with sympathetic understanding, a clear indication of his attitudes at the time. To Dublin he went at the bidding of mysterious voices in the Chelsea Road, according to his testimony, but certainly also at the urging of the not-so-mysterious Yeats and Martyn. There Moore finished *Sister Teresa,* the unsuccessful sequel to *Evelyn Innes;* collaborated with Yeats and Martyn on plays for the Irish theater; and bicycled through the Irish countryside with George Russell (AE) for whom he had a deep and lasting affection. Moore's identifiable contributions to the Irish Literary Theatre are *The Bending of the Bough* (a rewriting of Martyn's *The Tale of a Town*) , first printed in 1900, and *Diarmuid and Grania,* by George Moore and W. B.

Yeats, presented in 1901. His literary reputation, theatrical experience, and knowledge of stagecraft, however, contributed more than his name on these two plays might suggest—less, perhaps, than Moore claimed in *Hail and Farewell,* but substantially more than Yeats was later willing to acknowledge.

To those who thought of him as a follower of Zola, Moore's association with Yeats, Martyn, and Russell must have seemed curious. In the light of Moore's background it is not strange at all: Celtic mysticism was familiar to him from childhood; he had been brought up on Mayo legends, and Moore Hall had its own history of supernatural events. It was said in the family, for example, that on the day when Augustus Moore, George Henry's brother, died from injuries suffered in a racing accident, his ghost paid a farewell visit to his brother and cousin at Moore Hall. During George's childhood, it was not unusual for the ghost of his grandfather to appear to servants and family members. And Bridget Kelly, an old servant and the source of many of these accounts, had other tales to tell about the living and dead of the area. Moreover, in his childhood, Moore had had some instruction in Gaelic. Young George, of course, had paid little attention to learning the language, but Maurice apparently came to know it quite well. In any event, the echo-auguries that Moore credited with responsibility for the major changes in his life certainly were not the invention of a naturalist. In his writings, they are always related to water and birds, symbolic and portentous elements from Irish folk literature. Indeed, what passes for psychological interest in Moore's later works is often remarkably close to the personality changes, inner and outer compulsions, and related themes that abound in Irish folklore.

What Moore learned as a writer of the Irish Literary Renaissance, however, was not substance but method. The rhythmic prose that he had half tried under the influence of Pater and half developed under the guidance of Dujardin was polished and rewritten, polished and rewritten, until it had the natural rhythms of the practiced oral story teller. Meanwhile, the cold, dispassionate notes of the naturalist were replaced by a more perceptive understanding. For the disciple of Gautier, the visible world was still visible—but by 1901 Moore had come to believe that art was the visible world filtered through human perception. The task of the artist was to reveal not only the nature of the object perceived but also the mind and soul that perceived it.

In 1901, John Eglinton (W. K. Magee), one of the older advocates of the Irish Literary Revival, suggested that Moore undertake the writing of an Irish book patterned after Turgenev's *Tales of a Sportsman*. Moore, an admirer of Turgenev, was both flattered and astonished: "As well ask me to paint like Corot," he replied. Nevertheless, he began the series of stories (some appeared in the *New Ireland Review*) that was published in Irish in 1902 as *An T-Úr-Gort, Sgealta* by Seorsa O Morda (Moore's name in Gaelic). Moore himself did not know the language sufficiently to compose in it; the stories were translated from English. The following year they appeared in English under the title *The Untilled Field*—much improved, Moore maintained, for their bath in Irish. Of the original thirteen stories, some were later anthologized and translated into other languages. As a whole, Charles Morgan maintained, the collection was an example of "that ordered simplicity, that idealization of the rhythm of the speaking voice, which was the prose instrument that Moore invented and perfected."

Not all the stories in *The Untilled Field* deserve such unqualified praise. The Irish stories—sympathetically written tales of cottage and cleric—have a gentle, flowing style, varied yet repetitious, like the shadows of clouds, dappled with sunlight, that pass over a landscape. Less successful, the stories based on themes and character-types related to Moore's early work are stilted and awkward. The Dublin charwoman of "In the Clay," for example, greets the sculptor, Rodney, with news that someone has broken into his studio: " 'I'm afraid someone has been into the studio last night. The hasp was off the door when I came this morning. Some of the things are broken.' " Rodney examines the damage. It is extensive—the piece he hoped would be his prize sculpture has been destroyed. Remembering his plans, his hopes for the future, he exclaims: "Good Heavens! How happy I was yesterday, full of hope and happiness, my statue finished, and I going to meet Harding in Rome. The blow has fallen in the night. Who had done this? Who has destroyed my statue?' " Alice Barton, newly graduated from the convent of St. Leonard's, could not have written more amateurish speech into her graduation play.

In the Irish stories, emotions are more skillfully projected and dialogue is more appropriate. Rhythm and diction are more natural, better suited to the speaker. In addition, symbol and metaphor are handled more poetically. Bodies of water (lakes, canals, oceans) function as both landscape and symbol, as in Moore's later books. Word pictures are painted with specific reference to feelings, and the life of the body and the life of the imagination are shown as independent, two parallel streams that move toward one eternity. The shimmer of moonlight, for example, merges with the shimmer of imagined silk on the night of Margaret's death in "The Wedding Gown"; near the village from which Father Madden of "Julia Cahill's Curse" has driven away life, there are "scanty fields, drifting from thin grass into bog, and from bog into thin grass again, and in the distance a rim of melancholy mountains, and the peasants . . . seemed a counterpart of the landscape."

Moore's next novel—*The Lake,* published in 1905—originally was planned as a short story to be included in *The Untilled Field*. But as theme and character developed, Moore realized that it was a separate work, complete in itself yet linked stylistically with the stories of the collection, and for eighteen years it remained independent. In 1923 *The Untilled Field* and *The Lake* were reunited, published in a single volume in the Carra edition of Moore's works. (The Uniform edition and Ebury edition also print them together.)

As Moore explained in his preface to the revised (and much improved) edition of *The Lake* (1921), the story "passes within the priest's soul: it is tied and untied by the flux and reflux of sentiments, inherent in and proper to his nature"; it is "the weaving of a story out of the soul substance without ever seeking the aid of external circumstance." "To keep the story in the key in which it was conceived," wrote Moore, "it was necessary to recount the priest's life during the course of his walk by the shores of a lake, weaving his memories continually, without losing sight, however, of the long, winding, mere-like lake, wooded to its shores, with hills appearing and disappearing into mist and distance." The significance of the geography, in the drama intended to pass "within the priest's soul," is its relation to the "mysterious warble, soft as lake water, that abides in the heart." In *The Lake,* Moore wanted to present life not in breadth, but in depth, for "what counts in art is not width but depth."

The story opens in what at first appears to be conventional fashion: "It was one of those enticing days at the beginning of May when white clouds are drawn about the earth like curtains." The narrative voice seems to be omniscient. The main character of the novel, Father Oliver, appears. (Or has he been there all the time?) He walks along the shore of the lake, at the edge of the wood, and comes to a field; he is within sight of the headland that stretches into the lake. Neither field nor headland were mentioned in the opening paragraph of *The Lake;* only the immediate view—only that which could be seen by Father Oliver walking along the disused cart track—was described. An omniscient narrator does not tell us what is there, as it turns out; a character-narrator reveals what he is seeing. Throughout the entire story, with minor lapses, we are confined to his inner and

outer vision. In his mind's-eye view, no image of himself appears to him—nor, therefore, to us. Even when he
shaves, we cannot catch a glimpse of him, for he looks
not at himself but over the top of his mirror at his garden (and cuts his chin). The only clue to his physical
appearance is that which Moore presents through Father
Oliver's recollection or through the few comparisons
he makes between himself and others: As children, he
and his sister Eliza were the redhaired ones. (But is his
hair still red?) If he lives as long as Father Peter, who
died at fifty-five, he will live twenty-one more years by
the side of the lake. (He is therefore thirty-four.) These
facts are not even assembled for the reader, but are
widely scattered; they appear separately in passages
thirty-seven pages apart, punctuating Father Oliver's
thoughts and recollections about other matters.

Nevertheless, as the book unfolds, we know more
about Father Oliver than he knows about himself. For
example, we are able to assess his feelings toward Rose
Leicester (Nora Glynn in later editions) long before
he recognizes them. The technique is that of the modern novelist: We have access to correspondence and
conversations between Father Oliver and Father
O'Grady, Rose, and Eliza. We are able to make independent judgments based on what they write and say.
We can judge the data given us objectively, while Father
Oliver can make only subjective evaluations of himself.
Looking for clues, we can pick up and put together
thoughts that, to him, are disconnected.

In the first forty-one pages of the 1905 edition of *The
Lake*, Father Oliver's character is established, the his-

tory of his immediate family is told, his attitude toward
Ireland is described, his reasons for entering the priest-
hood are revealed, Rose Leicester's past (as much as he
knows of it) is reviewed, his feelings toward Rose are
hinted at—all through the medium of memory. The
lake, the wood, the weather, and natural objects provide scenes and objects that trigger his Proustian recall.
The sight of the headland, Derrinrush, leads to the
remembered smell of reeds and rushes and boyhood
play with a brother. A yacht on the lake stimulates wan-
derlust, which in turn reminds Father Oliver that almost
all his life has been spent within sight of the lake. The
Tinnick shoreline evokes thoughts of a sister, Eliza, now
mother superior of the Tinnick convent, and the town
where he was born. Thoughts of sister and birthplace
take him back along Lawrence Durrell's "iron links of
memory" to childhood, to a boyish attachment to Annie
McGrath, to his father's death and brother's emigration,
to his early plans to rebuild the mills of Tinnick, to his
romantic dreams of a hermitage on Castle Island, and
to his decision to become a priest. The yacht—which
Father Oliver has continued to watch throughout his
reverie—tacks toward Kilronan Abbey; his thoughts follow the same tack, mulling over the problems of the poor
people at the north end of the lake who used to be his
parishioners, comparing them with the people of his
present parish. Two members of his congregation,
women who were in church the Sunday he preached
against Rose Leicester, come down the path through
the juniper bushes. In his mind's ear he hears their
gossip—about him, he imagines, and how he has changed

since Rose left the district. And then the story that he admits he has tried to bar from his mind all morning rushes in on him. With it comes remorse, and a concentration on trees and bird habits to blunt its sharp edge. As Father Oliver's mood changes, with it changes his perception of the mood of the day.

Memory and observation provide the associations that structure this portion of *The Lake;* an exchange of letters between Father Oliver and Father O'Grady and Father Oliver and Rose Leicester adds the rest. Some of Father Oliver's memories result from his conscious attempts to recapture, but not relive, facts or fancies of days gone by. Some fly unbidden into his mind, bringing with them not only pictures and sounds from the past, but emotions and smells as well. Time is psychological: superimposed on the brief clock moments it takes to watch a yacht tack across a lake are years of memory. Eight pages are sufficient to describe a long but active evening with Father Moran during which Father Oliver tries to discourage his curate from drink, but more than ten full pages draw out a short visit on the night when Father Oliver awaits an opportunity to disappear from the parish. The lake is an actual lake; it is a symbolic lake, representing all that binds Father Oliver to his present circumstances; and it is the lake in his heart in which move the deep and restless currents unseen by others.

To say that George Moore used the techniques described above is not, however, to say that he used them expertly. The habits of omniscient authorship intrude: Moore comments philosophically on what passes through Father Oliver's mind during some of his walks along the lake; he cannot refrain from speaking in his own voice when Father Moran and Father Oliver take their first walk together. Again and again, method fails Moore in the first edition of *The Lake,* and he turns to letters to express the young priest's moods and feelings. Letters, however, inevitably contain a strong element of restraint and public awareness; they divert the current of Father Oliver's memories. When Moore resorts to letters, *The Lake* slips back into the old, familiar form of the epistolary novel. By 1921, when he revised *The Lake,* Moore had improved his subjective technique: the revision is a more effective work because it reduces the number of letters exchanged.

8
Last Novels
and Autobiographies:
Vision and Revision

The story of Moore's disenchantment with Ireland
has been told and retold from as many points of view as
there were articulate people involved. The two principle accounts of Moore's association with the Irish Literary Theatre are included, of course, in Moore's *Hail
and Farewell* and Yeats's *Autobiographies*. Both men
told their stories in retrospect, both were full of righ-
teous indignation, and both were eager to place whatever blame there was for things gone wrong where they
thought it rightly belonged—squarely on the shoulders
of others. Reports of their witty, insulting jibes at each
other spiced Dublin conversation for years after 1901,
when their collaborative efforts to produce a play based
on the legend of Diarmuid and Grania revealed irre-
concilable differences in attitudes toward art. Lady

Gregory, John Quinn, and others often tried to patch up their quarrels during and after the writing of the play, but little came of their efforts. *Diarmuid and Grania* was produced; it was not a success; each blamed the other for its failure; each felt that in the collaboration his aesthetic principles had been compromised. Reorganization of the Irish Literary Theatre in 1902 either forced or gave Moore an opportunity to withdraw from further projects involving joint efforts with Yeats. Since Moore and Martyn, who also withdrew from the Irish Literary Theatre at this time, got on no better than Moore and Yeats, there was no question of their cooperation, either, although Martyn had plans to continue his own work. Moore decided to devote his talents instead to *The Untilled Field*—and his influence to the work of the Gaelic League.

One of Douglas Hyde's Gaelic plays, *Casadh an t-Sugam* (*The Twisting of the Rope*) had been produced at Moore's invitation in his garden on Ely Place early in 1902; Moore had spoken publicly on several occasions in support of the language movement. Like most of Moore's enthusiasms, however, his efforts on behalf of the Irish language were overzealous, exaggerated to the point of foolishness, poorly received, and short lived. Certainly they were in no way assisted by his renunciation of Catholicism and espousal of Protestantism—which, in typical George Moore fashion, he made as public as possible.

By 1902 to 1903, in letters to Dujardin quoted by Joseph Hone, Moore was writing, "For the moment I've had enough of the Gaelic League" and "I have utterly renounced my Celtic aspirations" (Hone, *Life of George Moore,* pp. 244–45). Turning his back on Ireland, the Irish language, and things Irish as future subjects for his pen, he returned in the years 1903 to 1904 to his favorite subject: himself. A history of his literary and intellectual life, to be called *Avowals,* was planned and begun (although pieces were published in periodicals, they did not appear in book form until 1919). So was a history of his sentimental life, originally entitled "Moods and Memories" in articles printed in *Dana,* a new journal edited by John Eglinton; later (1906) published as *Memoirs of My Dead Life.* Meanwhile, having begun *The Lake,* Moore continued it—for his renunciation of Ireland did not include abandonment of a work of art.

In 1905 Moore was appointed High Sheriff of Mayo. Never one to refuse an honor or distinction, he of course accepted—besides, his disenchantment with Ireland was with Dublin intellectual circles and middle-class readers and playgoers, not with the people of Mayo. Moore Hall remained, as always, his "dreaming house." By August of 1905, his ceremonial duties having been fulfilled, Moore was in Paris. Continuing to threaten immediate departure from Ireland, he returned to Ely Place to write his farewell—to be called originally, according to a letter addressed to his brother Maurice dated 1906 (Hone, *Life of George Moore,* pp. 271–72), *Ave Hibernia! Atque Vale.* By 1907 the title had been changed to *Hail and Farewell,* and the new book was described as a novel in a letter to Dujardin, quoted by Hone (*Life of George Moore,* p. 273). Aware that Moore freely used fact when he was writing fiction and fiction when he was writing fact, Dublin was not comforted by the news. As Moore used to boast to AE, half of Dublin was afraid that they would appear as characters in the novel, the other half was afraid that they would not appear at all. Later, when Moore announced that his "novel" would contain real characters drawn from real life bearing their real names, anxiety in Dublin increased. Occasionally, as he finished portions of the manuscript, Moore would read aloud passages from it to his Saturday evening guests or would allow others to read selected pages—no doubt to keep Dublin in a state of anxiety and to retain the position he enjoyed as subject of much Dublin gossip. When the three volumes, *Ave, Salve,* and *Vale,* finally appeared in 1911 to 1914, Dublin was obligingly aghast.

Meanwhile, in the years between 1902 and 1910, Moore had become interested in writing a book about Christ and St. Paul. His imaginative curiosity had been aroused by Dujardin's *La Source du Fleuve Chrétien* (the title was translated as the title of Ralph Ellis's work in *The Lake*) ; it was increased by John Eglinton's talk of a new book about the historical Jesus, just received in the National Library. Moore's first attempt to handle the subject creatively was a scenario entitled *The Apostle,* originally printed in the *English Review* and subsequently expanded, as Edwin Gilcher notes, for publication by Maunsel (1911). His major work on the subject was, of course, *The Brook Kerith.*

In the preface to the New York edition of *The Brook Kerith,* published by Macmillan in 1916, Moore declared that the book was "derivative," "based on the many passages that seem to tell us that a pious Jew could not have done else but turn away horrified if any one of his disciples had asked him if he were the son of God, using the expression 'son of God' in the sense that it is used today in the churches." These lines would seem to indicate that the principal purpose of the novel was to recount the life of the historical Jesus, perhaps emphasizing his humanity and questioning his divinity. To be sure, such elements are present in *The Brook Kerith,* but they make up only a portion of the book.

The story begins with the childhood of Joseph of Arimathea. Samuel appears to him in a dream and tells him that he will be a prophet. The boy believes the dream; it has a profound effect upon him. Under the tender, understanding guidance of his father, Dan, he grows from an imaginative boy into a serious, intelligent, deeply religious young man. A trip to Jerusalem leads to acquaintance with the Essenes, a Jewish sect comprised solely of male members who live simple, chaste lives in a communal society near the Brook Kerith. Joseph joins them for a time, hoping to share their true spiritual exaltation: from Banu, a cave-dwelling prophet whom he visits at the suggestion of one of the Essenes, he hears that he "for whom the world is waiting" is at the River Jordan. Joseph hastens to the spot, and there, almost one hundred pages from the beginning of the book, he first hears the name of the new disciple of John the Baptist, Jesus the Essene. Joseph tries to find Jesus. He even journeys to Egypt after hearing that Jesus is there, but without success.

Back in Jerusalem once more, he becomes a prosperous trader, a man of importance. Pilate is his friend. Then, on a visit to his childhood home in Galilee, Joseph meets Jesus at last and immediately becomes one of his followers. In deference to old Dan, however, who is feeble and aged, and who fears that his son will be killed by Zealots, Joseph agrees to give up association with Jesus and the disciples, at least during Dan's lifetime. When he hears that Jesus has been condemned to die on the cross, however, he breaks his vow and rushes to Golgotha to try to save him. The centurion tells him that he is too late—there is no longer a life to save. Joseph asks his friend Pilate to release the body to him that he may give Jesus a proper burial. Over two hundred pages of the book have passed, and the focus is still on Joseph. The biblical events in the life of Jesus have been mentioned casually, only as they relate to the story of Joseph.

In the tomb, Jesus stirs. Joseph realizes that the centurion was mistaken: the crucified man has been wounded seriously, but he is not dead. In secret, Joseph and a trusted servant nurse Jesus back to health in Joseph's house. Jesus is humble and grateful; he does not speak of his past, and his only wish seems to be that he might remain with his benefactor. But the dangers of his being discovered in Jerusalem are too great, for both Joseph and Jesus, and Joseph finally arranges for Jesus to go back to the Essenes where he can return to his former tasks, shepherding his flock by the Brook Kerith. For a few pages the narrative is divided between Joseph and Jesus. Then, smoothly, it shifts to Jesus as

_____

the news is revealed in casual conversation that Joseph has been slain by Zealots in Jerusalem. Three-fifths of the novel has been completed at this point when the narration focuses on Jesus.

Jesus is a good shepherd; the flock, which had suffered during his absence, thrives under his care. He is a joyless man. The other Essenes notice that he rarely speaks and never smiles, and he seems to prefer the company of his sheep to that of men. Alone by the Brook Kerith, when Jesus thinks of God and his past life, it is to regret his blasphemous illusion, first that he was the Messiah, then that he was God. He tells himself that he has come to understand that "God is not here, nor there, but everywhere: in the flower, and in the star, and in the earth underfoot." To "gather the universal will into an image" and to call it God, however, seems to him to "drift back to the starting-point of all our misery," to become again "the dupes of illusion and desire." For "he who yields himself to God goes forth to persuade others to love God, and very soon his love of God impels him to violent words and cruel deeds. It cannot be else," Jesus tells himself, "for God is but desire, and whosoever yields to desire falls into sin. To be without sin we must be without God."

Jesus draws closer and closer to Eastern philosophy in the twenty-two years that he spends among the sheep of the Essenes. And then Paul arrives. He comes to the cenoby of the Essenes at night, fleeing the Jews who persecute him for his heretical beliefs. Paul tells the story of Jesus to the Essenes; at the same time, Jesus informs the leader of the sect that he has been guilty of blasphemy and must leave the cenoby. Paul thinks Jesus a madman; Jesus repents that his "folly has borne fruit." Together they journey toward Caesarea and Jerusalem, in strange fellowship—Paul to spread the story of Christ, Jesus to refute it. The focus of the narrative shifts once more, from Jesus to Paul. As Joseph's death was revealed in a few words of gossip, so Jesus is left standing on a hillside while the narrative continues with Paul to Caesarea, Celicia, Melita, Syracuse, Puteoli, and Rome.

Like so many of Moore's novels, *The Brook Kerith,* composed of the stories of Joseph, Jesus, and Paul, is tripartite in structure. But the form is not static as it is in the earlier novels. Like water, each portion of the narrative rises and falls rhythmically and flows into the next. The story of Joseph is a wave that begins with the dream of a child; it gathers force in the religious dedication of a young man; it breaks with his death. Behind it is another wave, the story of Jesus, sweeping upward. Behind it is still another, the story of Paul. And behind the story of Paul, beyond the horizon of the narrative, there are other waves, suggests the author, although they are not yet visible. The sense of flux is enhanced by the prose style in which description, dialogue, and the thought processes of the characters are all but currents in the same stream, not channeled into separate passages, not interrupted by such mechanical devices as quotation marks. James Joyce, who also sought the sense of flux and reflux in his writings, also discarded quotation marks; he substituted dashes and removed explanatory phrases. Not even dashes break up the flow of Moore's prose, but he retains the conventional "Joseph asked," "Azariah replied," and "Jesus answered," to keep the movement clear and the story intelligible.

Such clarity of narration is important because the outlines of the characters themselves are not clear. Joseph, Jesus, and Paul are not distinguishable by habits of speech or thought; they appear to be almost three phases of the same character. Sometimes, as in Virginia Woolf's *The Waves,* they seem to think each other's thoughts. At other times, they represent the reverse of the coin: the passivity of Jesus is opposed to the violence of Paul; the childhood and youth of Joseph is opposed to that of Jesus. As the three different modes of narration (description, dialogue, and internal monologue) flow together, so are the three main characters fused. On his first visit to the Essenes, Joseph learns the theory of Heraclitus from Mathias, and he is intrigued by it. Mathias himself has a mind that "moves in a rich erudite and complex syntax." His beautiful voice brings forth "sentence after sentence, like silk from off a spool." The language he speaks is Aramaic, which has long been familiar to Joseph, but never before has Joseph heard it spoken so beautifully. English has long been familiar to George Moore; for years he himself had struggled with modes of written expression, and he also had studied the techniques of others: never before, however, was he able to write so beautifully. Sentence after sentence, like the speeches of Mathias, the book unwinds, like silk from off a spool, maintaining a Heraclitean flux. Joseph, Jesus, and Paul all participate in

the creation of the Christ legend; they are the three
tributaries of that great ocean of belief. Heaven and
earth, god and man, all fuse into a pattern, and the pattern has motion that makes it eternally changing yet
eternally the same. Reading *The Brook Kerith,* George
Bernard Shaw was adversely affected by this quality of
the book. As he observed, there was no reason why
George Moore could not go on, in similar fashion,
through many more thousands of words in exactly the
same style and exactly the same manner. That the book
is a continuum, however, is evidence of its failure to
some and of its achievement to others. (In the same
way, conventional criticism found fault with the art of
the impressionists, which they saw as having no center,
no frame. The water paintings of Monet especially were
the butt of much humor by critics who professed an
inability to tell right from left, top from bottom, of his
"formless" studies of water, sky, and reflections.)

The effect Moore was seeking in *A Brook Kerith,*
according to statements printed in *Avowals,* was that
of "a tale by Turgenev . . . or a landscape by Corot."
These, he declared, were "the holy places where I rested
and rest; together they have revealed to me all that I
needed to know." The result was a style uniquely his
own. He had listened to Manet, Degas, the impressionists, Turgenev, and Corot, as he later told a friend, but
he did not take all that they said for gospel: he was
George Moore, with something to say for himself.

The years Moore had spent in France had been important to the development of his style, however: that
much is clear. Although in French, as in English, he

was sloppy about grammar, his sensitive ear picked up
the rhythm and pattern of French speech. "S'il arraivait
à Moore de commetre de grossières erreurs de gram-
maire," writes Collet, "il n'en est pas moins vrai qu'il
était capable d'utiliser notre langue avec infinement de
finesse." Moore's prefatory letter of dedication to
Edouard Dujardin, at the beginning of *The Lake* indicates his fluency in the language. Rereading what he
had written, Geraint Goodwin reports, Moore was
struck by the beauty of the long sentences, the descriptions of the Seine, the poplar trees, the swallows flying
low over the water. It was this style, says Goodwin (*Conversations with George Moore*, p. 121), that Moore determined to develop in English.

Pattern and rhythm sometimes reminiscent of French
idiom characterize the prose of Moore's last novels.
Rhythm in prose, as defined by E. M. Forster, is repetition plus variation—a unifying device, but one that leads
to an opening out rather than a rounding off of a work.
It should not always be present, says Forster, but should
wax and wane, filling the reader "with surprise and
hope." In the French epistle that he had written to
Dujardin, Moore had heard the rhythmic rise and fall
of the dependent clauses, the muted expression of
thought, subtly projective, yet paradoxically echoing
what had been said before. The style is reflective, flowing; it has the sense of unhurried motion that is at the
same time an excellence and a fault in Moore's later
writings. The long digressions of his last novel, *Aphrodite in Aulis*, for example, were considered by Charles
Morgan to be structural flaws; Humbert Wolfe, how-

ever, found structural unity in the narrative method
that "glances from thought to thought, from memory to
memory, and through emotion after emotion"—a
method, he says, that anticipated both Proust and Joyce.
In the prose of *The Brook Kerith* (1916), *Heloise and
Abelard* (1921), *Ulick and Soracha* (1926), and *Aphrodite in Aulis* (1930), the unhurried, rhythmic effect is
achieved through repetition and assonance and through
the natural cadences of cultured English speech sprin-
kled with archaisms, especially those constructions in
which the inflection rises slightly at the end of a clause.
The narrative is composed of sensuous lines that wind
in and out and around characters and events in a rhythmic pattern that stops but does not end. Sounds and
words are repeated within each passage to provide
rhythm. The style is consciously artistic, a combination
of techniques drawn from Moore's experiences as artist
and art critic, from the musical devices he learned from
Dujardin, and from the prose of Pater.

As Moore repeats sounds and words in a passage to
give it rhythm, so does he create events that recur and
people that reappear, in the larger narrative, to establish
pattern. It is the story that appeals to curiosity and the
plot to intelligence, according to Forster, but it is pa-
tern that appeals to the aesthetic sense. Pattern, of
course, had been a major concern of Moore's in his
early work, but it had been applied artificially. The pattern of Moore's later novels is organic, related to rhythm
in sentence and paragraph, serving the author's syner-
gistic vision. It is constructed in part from the recurrent
use of characteristic symbols: the nest of rooks, or other

birds; the lake, stream, or other body of water. Within
the first seventy pages of *Aphrodite in Aulis* (published in 1930), for example, the following references
to water may be found: leaving Athens, Kebren hears
the "mysterious sound" of the Kephosos under its
oleanders; he is on his way to see the Bay of Aulis from
which the Greeks sailed to Troy; he follows the sound
of running water to its source; he awakens on the
wharves of the Bay of Aulis, having fallen asleep without knowing where he was; at the house of Otanes, he is
attracted by the statue of the River God, which spouts
in the middle of the court; he has a deep interest in the
story of Leda bathing in the river, where she was visited
by Zeus as a swan; he dreams of giving a lecture on the
banks of the Eurotas, and then awakens as "quietly as
an otter sliding into the water"; once more he studies
the River God and surrounding related sculpture and
mosaics in the courtyard of Otanes; the dreams of
Otanes, says Kebren, will "rise up again like a river";
the draining of Lake Kopais is debated; an early morning boat trip up the river is described; near a brook that
flows with a drowsy murmur, Kebren and Biote talk,
"their speech taking tune from the water"; walking together, they come across a pool in which maidens are
splashing; the tapestry that Biote's mother was working
on when she died showed Diana's nymphs bathing,
watched by Actaeon; walking along the shore, Kebren
speculates to Biote that perhaps the waves are like generations, the bubbles on the foam like men and women.
Years before the writing of *Aphrodite in Aulis,* in the
1916 edition of *Confessions of a Young Man,* Moore

announced, "I fain would show my soul in these pages, like a face in a pool of clear water."

Sentences in *The Brook Kerith, Heloise and Abelard, Ulick and Soracha,* and *Aphrodite in Aulis* wind back on themselves, then spiral out again in new clauses; characters weave in and out of the narrative; the rooks rise from the nest in ever-widening circles; in the smooth water of the bay, which meets the curve of the beach, the soft, sinuous roll of the hills is reflected. Everywhere the serpentine line is evident, recalling the contrast of curve and angle in *A Mummer's Wife* and the aesthetic theories of harmonious line that had been established by such artists of the past as Hogarth, Delacroix, and Ingres, and that had been adopted by later painters in both England and France. Each of the later novels ends, not with a conclusion, but with an unfinished curve, left to fall and rise again in the pattern that had been established. In *The Brook Kerith*, Paul is left at the end of a day in which he has expounded on the kingdom of God and the birth, death, and resurrection of Jesus; another day, clearly, will follow: "He spoke from morning to evening," writes Moore in the penultimate paragraph. The last paragraph is composed of one line only: "The rest of the story is unknown." But the suggestion is clear: there was more. Similarly in *Heloise and Abelard* the lovers are left riding toward Troyes. The rest of their story, Moore says, is a matter of record: so there was more. Rhesos and Earine, at the end of *Aphrodite in Aulis*, hasten to Aulis: "Already the company may be wondering at our absence," says Earine, "and I am looking forward to seeing the sculptor of

Aphrodite and the builder of her temple stand side by side to receive the homage that is their due." Under the greenwood, by the Bay of Aulis, they have just conceived a child. So, once again, there was more.

As Moore's last novels indicate, style, not story, was his chief concern during the final years of his life. Friends have reported that he revised endlessly, often beating out the rhythm of his long, winding sentences with his hand as he tested passages he had recently committed to paper. His goal was to recreate the flowing, musical, incantatory prose of the oral storyteller, and often he would struggle for days to find the exact word —one that would provide the tonal quality he desired as well as the meaning he wished to communicate.

For such prose Moore needed appropriate characters. The modern, urbane, witty men and women drawn from Dublin life whom he set in verbal opposition to himself and others in *Hail and Farewell* would not do. The style he wished to develop was ancient, noble, dignified: his characters must be, too. Nor was he interested any longer in contriving action. Most of *The Lake* was in the lapping of waves of memory against the mind of Father Gogarty. Father Gogarty's meetings with others often halted his story temporarily rather than contributing to its purpose.

History and legend provided Moore with the new subjects he needed for his new style. Thus *The Brook Kerith* was based on accounts of the life of the historical Jesus, with Joseph of Arimathea as the character in focus; *A Story-Teller's Holiday,* an exchange of playful, irreverent stories between an Anglo-Irish George Moore and a Mayo fern gatherer, was woven out of Mayo legend and practices associated with Irish monastic discipline; *Heloise and Abelard,* Moore's much praised novel of the middle ages, was based on the letters of the famous lovers; *The Pastoral Loves of Daphnis and Chloe* was a translation of a story by Longus, for the most part from the French of Jacques Amyot; *Perronik the Fool* was a retelling of an old Breton legend; *Ulick and Soracha* was suggested by incidents from the history of the Bruce invasion that involved Carra Castle; and *Aphrodite in Aulis* was a blending of themes, thoughts, characters, events, and places out of history and old mythologies artfully worked into a story set in fifth-century Greece.

Perhaps it was Moore's fascination with oral narration during the last twenty years of his life that increased his interest in writing for the stage. In any case, the period is marked by publication of a number of plays: *Esther Waters* (1913), a skillful dramatization of his most successful novel; *Elizabeth Cooper* (1913), a clever little comedy that makes use once again of a character so unsure of himself that he must borrow the identity of another; *The Coming of Gabrielle* (1920), a revision of *Elizabeth Cooper; The Apostle* (1923), a dramatization of a portion of *The Brook Kerith* (not to be confused with *The Apostle* of 1911, which was little more than a scenario); *The Making of an Immortal* (1927), a humorous tale of an unscrupulous Shakespeare who steals all credit for plays actually written by Bacon and others; *The Passing of the Essenes* (1930), a revision of *The Apostle* as it appeared in

1923. Although never a successful dramatist, Moore was by no means a failure: many of his plays were quite well received, and critics noted particularly his gift for clever dialogue. To what degree the dialogue was his is a matter that invites scholarly investigation. It was no secret that Moore openly sought help in constructing his plays, although the equal responsibility of collaboration usually was too much for him to allow to another.

Moore's interest in oral narration is evident during the last period of his life not only in his last prose style and in the plays of the period but also in the structure of his autobiographical works. Instead of writing reminiscences in the privacy of his library, he preferred to dictate recollections of conversations—real or imaginary—to a secretary. *Conversations on Ebury Street* (1924) was, as a result, more personal than his earlier autobiographies; in it Moore seems to be facing his readers directly rather than allowing them to look in through the window of his mind. His last autobiographical fragment—*A Communication to My Friends* (1933)—has a similar quality, although Moore did not live to complete it or to revise and polish, in his usual fashion, those parts that were written before his death.

Revision and rewriting of earlier works occupied much of Moore's time during the last years of his life, perhaps interfering with the development of new ideas he hoped to add to his canon. As Edwin Gilcher has indicated in his excellent bibliography, minor revisions were introduced almost every time a work was reprinted, and some books were revised extensively, although their titles were unchanged. Two that were rewritten and published under new titles in the last years of Moore's life were *A Modern Lover,* which became *Lewis Seymour and Some Women* in 1917, and *A Drama in Muslin,* published merely as *Muslin* in 1915. But, as previously noted, *The Lake,* originally published in 1905, was much changed and much improved by the time the 1921 edition was sent to the press, although its title remained the same, and in an appendix to the Riverside edition published by Houghton Mifflin in 1963 Lionel Stevenson has carefully detailed the differences that mark the various editions of *Esther Waters.*

Much more attention needs to be given to Moore's habits of writing and revision before any accurate assessment of his position in the literary world of 1873 to 1933 can be made. Moore himself has left us with enough statements equating correction and virtue to suggest, even without bibliographical evidence, that such a study should be made. With bibliographical evidence, its importance becomes obvious, for not until the task begun by Royal A. Gettman ("George Moore's Revisions of *The Lake,* 'The Wild Goose,' and *Esther Waters,*" *PMLA,* June, 1944) is completed, can we begin to answer the questions asked by Graham Owens in his preface to *George Moore's Mind and Art.* For the present, Moore's position is assured. His writings reflect central literary trends of his time, his experiments in technique reveal a creative mind at work, and—as more and more readers are discovering—George Moore produced a significant number of short stories, novels, and autobiographical works of enduring literary quality.

Selected Bibliography

Note: No attempt has been made here to list all the works of George Moore, including essays, reviews, sketches, and stories published in periodicals: space simply would not permit. Nor has there been any attempt to distinguish re-written versions of previously published works issued under new titles: this information is supplied in the text. Interested readers who wish more bibliographical information than is included here may consult Edwin Gilcher's excellent new bibliography (see entry below).

I. BOOKS AND PLAYS BY GEORGE MOORE
(First Editions, in Order of Publication)

Flowers of Passion. London: Provost & Co., 1878.

Martin Luther: A Tragedy in Five Acts. London: Remington & Co., 1879.

Pagan Poems. London: Newman & Co., 1881.

A Modern Lover. London: Tinsley Brothers, 1883.

A Mummer's Wife. London: Vizetelly and Company, 1885.

Literature at Nurse. London: Vizetelly and Company, 1885.

A Drama in Muslin. London: Vizetelly and Company, 1886.

A Mere Accident. London: Vizetelly and Company, 1887.

Parnell and His Island. London: Swan Sonnenschein, Lowrey and Company, 1887.

Confessions of A Young Man. London: Swan Sonnenschein, Lowrey and Company, 1888.

Spring Days. London: Vizetelly and Company, 1888.

Mike Fletcher. London: Ward and Downey, 1889.

Impressions and Opinions. London: David Nutt, 1891.

Vain Fortune. London: Henry and Company, 1891.

Modern Painting. London: Walter Scott, Limited, 1893.

The Strike at Arlingford. London: Walter Scott, Limited, 1893.

Esther Waters. London: Walter Scott, Limited, 1894.

Celibates. London: Walter Scott, Limited, 1895.

Evelyn Innes. London: T. Fisher Unwin, 1898.

The Bending of the Bough. London: T. Fisher Unwin, 1900.

Sister Teresa. London: T. Fisher Unwin, 1901.

The Untilled Field. London: T. Fisher Unwin, 1903.

The Lake. London: William Heinemann, 1905.

Memoirs of My Dead Life. London: William Heinemann, 1906.

The Apostle: A Drama in Three Acts. Dublin: Maunsel and Company, 1911.

Hail and Farewell: Ave. London: Heinemann and Company, 1911; *Salve.* London: Heinemann and Company, 1912; *Vale.* London: Heinemann and Company, 1914.

Esther Waters: A Play. London: Heinemann and Company, 1913.

Elizabeth Cooper. Dublin and London: Maunsel and Company, 1913.

Muslin. London: William Heinemann and Company, 1915.

The Brook Kerith: A Syrian Story. London: T. Werner Laurie, 1916.

Lewis Seymour and Some Women. New York: Brentano's, 1917.

A Story-Teller's Holiday. London: Cumann Sean-eolais na h-Eireann, 1918. (Note: These and other books, privately printed by Moore, bear the same imprint; no such society as "Cumann Sean-eolais na h-Eireann" existed, however, as Edwin Gilcher points out in his bibliography.)

Avowals. London: Cumann Sean-eolais na h-Eireann, 1919.

The Coming of Gabrielle. London: Cumann Sean-eolais na h-Eireann, 1920.

Heloise and Abelard. London: Cumann Sean-eolais na h-Eireann, 1921.

In Single Strictness. London: William Heinemann, 1922.

Conversations on Ebury Street. London: William Heinemann, 1924.

Pure Poetry: An Anthology. London: Nonesuch Press, 1924.

The Pastoral Loves of Daphnis and Chloe. London: William Heinemann, 1924.

Daphnis and Chloe, Perronik the Fool. New York: Boni and Liveright, 1924.

Ulick and Soracha. London: Nonesuch Press, 1926.

Celibate Lives. London: William Heinemann, 1927.

The Making of an Immortal. New York: Bowling Green Press, 1927; London: Faber and Gwyer, Limited, 1927.

The Passing of the Essenes: A Drama in Three Acts. London: William Heinemann, 1930.

Aphrodite in Aulis. New York: Fountain Press, 1930.

A Flood. New York: Harbor Press, 1930.

The Talking Pine. Paris: Hours Press, 1931.

A Communication to My Friends. London: Nonesuch Press, 1933.

Diarmuid and Grania: A Play in Three Acts. With W. B. Yeats. *Dublin Magazine,* April–June, 1951.

II. COLLECTED EDITIONS

Carra Edition. 21 vols. New York: Boni and Liveright, 1922–24.

Uniform Edition. 20 vols. London: William Heinemann, 1924–33.

Ebury Edition. 20 vols. London: William Heinemann, 1937.

III. LETTERS BY GEORGE MOORE
(In Order of Publication)

Moore Versus Harris. Detroit: Privately printed for subscribers, 1921.

Letters to Dujardin. New York: Crosby Gaige, 1929.

Letters of George Moore [to John Eglinton]. Bournemouth: Privately printed, 1942.

Letters to Lady Cunard. Edited by Rupert Hart-Davis. London: Rupert Hart-Davis, 1957.

George Moore in Transition. Edited by Helmut E. Gerber. Detroit: Wayne State University Press, 1968.

IV. BIOGRAPHIES AND CRITICAL STUDIES: A SELECTED LIST

Archer, William. *Real Conversations.* London: William Heinemann, 1904.

Blanche, Jacques Émile. *Portraits of a Lifetime.* Translated by Walter Clement. New York: Coward McCann, 1933.

Brown, Malcolm. *George Moore: A Reconsideration.* Seattle: University of Washington Press, 1955.

Clark, Barrett H. "George Moore." *Intimate Portraits.* New York: Dramatists Play Service, 1951.

Collet, Georges-Paul. *George Moore et la France.* Paris and Geneva: E. Droz, 1957.

Cunard, Nancy. *GM: Memories of George Moore*. London: Rupert Hart-Davis, 1956.

Eglinton, John. *Irish Literary Portraits*. London: Macmillan, 1935.

Ervine, St. John. *Some Impressions of My Elders*. New York: Macmillan, 1922.

Ferguson, Walter D. *The Influence of Flaubert on George Moore*. Philadelphia: University of Pennsylvania Press, 1934.

Freeman, John. *A Portrait of George Moore in a Study of His Work*. London: T. Werner Laurie, Limited, 1922.

Gettman, Royal A. "George Moore's Revisions of *The Lake*, 'The Wild Goose,' and *Esther Waters*." *PMLA* 59 (June, 1944) : 540–55.

Goodwin, Geraint. *Conversations with George Moore*. New York: Alfred A. Knopf, 1930.

Harris, Frank. *Contemporary Portraits*. 2nd Series. New York: Printed by the author, 1919.

Hicks, Granville. *Figures of Transition*. New York: Macmillan, 1939.

Hone, Joseph Maunsell. *The Life of George Moore,* with an account of his last years by his cook and housekeeper, Clara Warville. New York: Macmillan, 1936.

———. *The Moores of Moore Hall*. London: Jonathan Cape, 1939.

Hough, Graham. "George Moore and the Nineties." *Edwardians and Late Victorians*. Edited by Richard Ellmann. English Institute Essays, 1959; New York: Columbia University Press, 1960.

———. *The Last Romantics*. London: Gerald Duckworth and Company, 1949.

Howarth, Herbert. *The Irish Writers 1880–1940*. London: Rockliff, 1958.

Hughes, Douglas A. *The Man of Wax: Critical Essays on*

George Moore. New York: New York University Press, 1971.

MacCarthy, Desmond. *Portraits*. London: Putnam, 1932.

Mitchell, Susan. *George Moore*. Dublin and London: Maunsel and Company, 1916.

Moore, Maurice. *An Irish Gentleman: George Henry Moore*. London: T. Werner Laurie, 1913.

Morgan, Charles. *Epitaph on George Moore*. New York: Macmillan, 1935.

Nejdefors-Frisk, Sonja. *George Moore's Naturalistic Prose*. Upsala Irish Studies, no. 3, edited by S. B. Lillegren. Upsala: Lundequist, 1952.

Noel, Jean C. *George Moore: l'Homme et l'Oeuvre (1852–1933)*. Paris: Didier, 1966.

Owens, Graham, ed. *George Moore's Mind and Art*. New York: Barnes and Noble, 1970.

Sechler, Robert Porter. *George Moore: A Disciple of Walter Pater*. Philadelphia: University of Pennsylvania Press, 1931.

Wolfe, Humbert. *George Moore*. London: H. Shaylor, 1931.

Yeats, William Butler. *The Autobiography of W. B. Yeats*. New York: Doubleday Anchor Books, 1958.

V. BIBLIOGRAPHY

Gilcher, Edwin. *A Bibliography of George Moore*. DeKalb, Illinois: Northern Illinois University Press, 1970.

Index